Tolley's
Client Tax Planning:
A Guide for Financial Advisers
and Practitioners
2002–2003

by Jim Hawkins, BSc

Members of the LexisNexis Group worldwide

United Kingdom	LexisNexis Butterworths Tolley, a Division of Reed Elsevier (UK) Ltd, Halsbury House, 35 Chancery Lane, LONDON, WC2A 1EL, and 4 Hill Street, EDINBURGH EH2 3JZ
Argentina	LexisNexis Argentina, BUENOS AIRES
Australia	LexisNexis Butterworths, CHATSWOOD, New South Wales
Austria	LexisNexis Verlag ARD Orac GmbH & Co KG, VIENNA
Canada	LexisNexis Butterworths, MARKHAM, Ontario
Chile	LexisNexis Chile Ltda, SANTIAGO DE CHILE
Czech Republic	Nakladatelství Orac sro, PRAGUE
France	Editions du Juris-Classeur SA, PARIS
Hong Kong	LexisNexis Butterworths, HONG KONG
Hungary	HVG-Orac, BUDAPEST
India	LexisNexis Butterworths, NEW DELHI
Ireland	Butterworths (Ireland) Ltd, DUBLIN
Italy	Giuffrè Editore, MILAN
Malaysia	Malayan Law Journal Sdn Bhd, KUALA LUMPUR
New Zealand	LexisNexis Butterworths, WELLINGTON
Poland	Wydawnictwo Prawnicze LexisNexis, WARSAW
Singapore	LexisNexis Butterworths, SINGAPORE
South Africa	Butterworths SA, DURBAN
Switzerland	Stämpfli Verlag AG, BERNE
USA	LexisNexis, DAYTON, Ohio

© Reed Elsevier (UK) Ltd 2002

A CIP Catalogue record for this book is available from the British Library.

ISBN 0 75451 868 X

Typeset by Marie Armah-Kwantreng, Dublin
Printed and bound in Great Britain by Hobbs the Printers Ltd, Totton, Hampshire

Visit Butterworths LexisNexis *direct* at www.butterworths.com

About this book

Originally, personal tax advice was dispensed by the family solicitor. This role was then taken over by accountants. However, most individuals do not employ an accountant either to deal with their tax affairs, or obtain tax advice.

Research by KPMG forecasts that private wealth will rise to £1,000 billion by 2003 – a rise of some 66% since 2001. This means that more and more people find they have capital or surplus income to invest. Many of them will turn to a financial adviser.

There is great scope, therefore, for a financial adviser to offer tax mitigation advice. There are two main benefits for them. Firstly, giving this advice helps them to build up a good relationship with their clients where they can be seen not just to be promoting products. As clients come to depend on their financial advisers, a long-term relationship is built-up, rather as with a family solicitor.

Secondly, although the advice is not specifically product-orientated, it will inevitably generate business. There is a third benefit which pertains to fee-based financial advisers in that they can, of course, charge fees for their advice and thus generate income.

As clients become more demanding, it will be necessary to be aware of an increasing range of possible solutions to their tax problems. The aim of this book is to make financial advisers and practitioners aware of some of the possibilities which exist to reduce clients' actual or potential taxation burdens.

It is based on a combination of the author's experience in writing about personal financial topics from a tax angle, and from extensive desk research in the many LexisNexis Butterworths Tolley publications which deal with all aspects of personal taxation in an extremely comprehensive way.

This is a slim volume by design – the aim is not to put the reader in a position to pass an examination in tax theory, rather to make them aware of the practical possibilities which exist. It is a distillation from many sources.

LexisNexis publications which have been particularly useful are:

Tolley's Tax Guide 2001–02;

RSM Robson Rhodes Personal Planning Manual 2001–02;

About this book

Offshore Tax Planning (Tolley's International);

Estate Planning 2001–02 (Tolley's);

Ray's Practical Inheritance Tax Planning;

Taxation of the Family (Butterworths);

Offshore Strategies (Tolley's International);

Simon's Tax Planning.

Many of the ideas in this book are more fully discussed therein in much greater detail.

The following weekly magazines, published by Tolley, have also proved invaluable sources of reference:

Taxation;

The Tax Journal.

The majority of suggestions rely on tax law which is the same throughout the UK. In certain cases – particularly concerning wills, divorce and cohabitation – information is based on the law in England and Wales.

Unless otherwise stated, the tax rates, allowances etc. cited in this book are those applying in 2002–03.

Finally, this book is dedicated to my father, whose keen interest in personal finance was the catalyst which encouraged me to start researching and writing in this area.

Contents

Contents

Abbreviations

AVCs	=	Additional voluntary contributions
AIMs	=	Alternative investment market
CGT	=	Capital gains tax
EIS	=	Enterprise investment scheme
FSA	=	Financial Services Authority
FURBS	=	Funded unapproved retirement benefit scheme
GRY	=	Gross redemption yield
IHT	=	Inheritance tax
PIB	=	Permanent interest-bearing shares
PET	=	Potentially exempt transfer
PPR	=	Principal private residence
SIPP	=	Self-invested personal pension
SSAS	=	Small self-administered scheme
TEPs	=	Traded endowment policies
VCTs	=	Venture capital trusts

Chapter 1

The Basic Tax System

Introduction

1.1 One of the basic principles of tax mitigation is to ensure that all individuals fully utilise the tax allowances that are available to them. A necessary background to this is an understanding of how the tax system works. What follows is a basic description so far as it impinges on this basic principle. It is not a comprehensive description of the tax system and all the available allowances.

General principles of income tax

1.2 UK residents are generally liable to income tax on all their income, whether it arises in the UK or abroad. We shall concern ourselves with those who are ordinarily resident in the UK. Each individual, including children, is liable in their own right, although, as we shall see later, a child's income may be treated as a parent's in certain circumstances.

1.3 All individuals are entitled to a personal allowance. In the current tax year 2002–03 this is £4,615, rising to £6,100 for those aged 65 to 74 and £6,370 for those aged 75 and over. These higher rates are subject to a claw-back if income exceeds a certain limit. There are additional allowances for certain married couples – these are explained later.

1.4 The rate of income tax payable depends upon the type of income. There are three different types – interest-bearing savings income, dividends from shares and non-savings income.

1.5 In the current tax year, after personal allowances, the first £1,920 of income from whatever source is charged to tax at the lower rate of 10%. The basic rate tax band runs from £1,921 up to £29,900. Interest-bearing savings income within this band is charged at 20%, usually deducted at source, and non-savings income at 22%. Dividend income within this band is paid over net of basic rate tax, which is deemed to be 10%. This means that a net dividend received of £90 is treated as if it were a gross dividend before tax of £100.

1.6 All income net of personal allowances above £29,900 is subject to the higher rate of tax. This is 40% for interest-bearing savings income and non-savings income. Therefore, interest-bearing savings income which has been paid over net of basic rate tax, will be subject to a further 20% charge.

1.7 In the case of dividend income, the higher rate is 32.5%. So, a gross dividend of, say, £100 is subject to £32.50 tax in total. Since £10 is deemed to have been already paid, a further £22.50 is due. This actually represents 25% of the net dividend received of £90. Thus, the simplest way to work out the liability to higher rate tax on dividend income is to take 25% of net dividends received.

General principles of capital gains tax

1.8 We shall concern ourselves first with capital gains tax (CGT) as it relates to non-business assets, confining ourselves to shares in any company other than the one for which an individual is an employee. Essentially, CGT is payable on the amount of any gain realised when shares are sold. Any capital losses can be set off against chargeable gains, and carried forward if unrelieved.

1.9 The first £7,700 of an individual's net gains is exempt – the annual exempt amount. The balance is taxed as income and charged at either 10% or 20% to the extent that an individual's total taxable income (including the capital gain) is within the starting rate band or basic rate band. If the gain takes income into the higher rate band, it is charged at 40%. The annual exempt amount is only available in the year to which it relates – it cannot be carried forward if unutilised.

1.10 For shares acquired prior to 6 April 1998 the inflationary element of any gain is removed by adjusting the purchase price for inflation up to that date – indexation. From 6 April 1998 onwards, taper relief applies whereby the chargeable gain is reduced by 5% once the shares have been held for three full years, increasing in steps of 5% per annum up to a maximum of 40% when they have been held for ten or more full years. In addition, shares acquired before 17 March 1998 qualify for their first 5% of taper relief a year earlier – from 6 April 2000.

1.11 In order to match sales with purchases, shares purchased on or after 6 April 1998 will be presumed to be sold on a last in first out basis. Shares acquired between the 6 April 1982 and 5 April 1998 will be pooled and deemed to be sold next, followed by shares acquired between 6 April 1965 and 5 April 1982, in both cases without identifying any particular shares in those holdings. Last in line are shares held on 6 April 1965, again on a last in first out basis.

1.12   There are special rules to deal with shares bought back within 30 days of disposal. Such transactions are matched to avoid the artificial establishment of a gain at the end of a tax year by selling shares on 5 April and buying them back on 6 April – 'bed and breakfasting'.

1.13   With scrip issues (free shares allocated to existing shareholders) and rights issues (the right for existing shareholders to subscribe to further shares at a favourable price) the shares are deemed to have been acquired on the same date as the actual shares to which the scrip or rights issue applies. Any taper relief available is applied to the total acquisition cost, including the cost of any rights, right back to the date of the original acquisition. Indexation relief, where applicable, can only, however, be applied to the rights portion from the date it was taken up.

1.14   It is important to establish the correct order in which to deal with gains.

- Establish the actual gain by deducting the purchase price, adjusted for any indexation which applies, from the sale price.

- Set off any losses that are suffered in the same tax year, and then any losses that are brought forward from earlier years. The allocation of losses to gains will be on the basis which produces the lowest tax charge. This means that the taxpayer can set off losses against gains which qualify for the least amount of taper relief. Even if losses in the same year reduce a gain below the level of the annual exempt amount, they must still be applied. In the case of losses brought forward, it is only necessary to apply sufficient to reduce total gains down to the annual exempt amount.

- Apply any taper relief which is available.

- If total tapered gains exceed the annual exempt amount, deduct the annual exempt amount from them.

1.15   It is clear from the above that if a financial adviser is going to advise a client about CGT mitigation they will need to have full details of the client's share portfolio in order to ascertain the size of any potential CGT liability.

1.16   As far as business assets are concerned the taper relief regime is much more favourable. Only 50% of any gain is chargeable once an asset has been held for one year, dropping to 25% once it has been held for two years or more.

General principles of inheritance tax

1.17   Inheritance Tax (IHT) is the most avoidable of all the personal taxes. In essence, it is payable on the size of an individual's net personal estate at the date of their death. The first £250,000 is exempt – the nil rate band – and the balance is charged at a flat rate of 40%. The other most common occasion when IHT might become payable, is during the lifetime of an individual, when transfers in excess of the nil rate band are made into a discretionary trust.

1.18   No CGT is payable on death – all assets liable to it are revalued at market value at the date of death, but this does not give rise to a CGT charge. The principle here is that the same gain cannot be charged to tax twice, and IHT takes precedence. Assets are transferred to beneficiaries at market value at date of death, and that is the base cost as far as the beneficiaries are concerned.

1.19   Many gifts made during lifetime are completely exempt from tax, and these are detailed later.

Chapter 2

Basic Mitigation of Income Tax

Non-taxpayers

2.1   If an individual's taxable income does not exceed their personal allowance, there will be no liability to income tax. In most cases where tax is deducted at source, this can be reclaimed, but it is often possible to arrange interest to be paid gross. In the case of some National Savings products, particularly investment accounts, ordinary accounts, income bonds, capital bonds and pensioners' bonds, income is always paid gross.

2.2   Income from banks, building societies and annuities can be paid gross by lodging form R85 with the provider. Similarly, by going through the National Savings stock register an investor can arrange to receive gross interest on any investment in Government securities – gilts.

2.3   Tax credits on UK dividends cannot be reclaimed. The natural inference here is that non-taxpayers should keep their investments in interest-bearing products. In most cases this is almost certainly true, but it must be borne in mind that such a strategy removes the possibility of any appreciation of capital.

Pensions and ISAs

2.4   Turning now to those paying tax, the two most significant basic ways of reducing tax are via individual savings accounts (ISAs) and pension contributions. The current annual ISA allowance is £7,000 and pension contributions are governed by level of income. As far as ISAs are concerned, no more than £3,000 can be allocated to a cash component and no more than £1,000 may be allocated to an insurance component in any year. There is no separate limit for a stocks and shares component, so any amount up to £7,000 may be allocated to that component.

2.5   Company employees may have access to an occupational pension scheme. Maximum contributions here are 15% of salary up to a maximum of £97,200 net relevant earnings. Occupational schemes typically require an employee to contribute anything up to 9% of salary. Three options exist to make further contributions, subject to the limits mentioned. The first is to make additional voluntary contributions (AVCs) to the employer's scheme if such a facility exists. The second is to make contributions to a separate scheme – free-standing AVCs.

2.6 The third, for those who have earned £30,000 or less in at least one of the tax years from 2000-01 onwards, and have not been controlling directors in the same period, is to make contributions to a stakeholder pension, up to a limit of £2,808 per year. These stakeholder contributions will be grossed up by the Inland Revenue as if they had been paid net of basic rate tax. Thus the maximum contribution of £2,808 will be topped up to £3,600.

2.7 The stakeholder and AVC routes are likely to be better options than free-standing AVCs, since charges will almost certainly be significantly higher in the latter case.

2.8 Those who are self-employed or who are not members of an occupational scheme can contribute to a personal pension, which can be a stakeholder. Contributions up to £2,808 are not earnings related, and are grossed up regardless of the contributor's income. After that, tax relief depends upon income, subject to the same overall cap as an occupational scheme, and based on a percentage of net relevant earnings, starting at 17.5% for those aged 35 or less, rising to 20% for those aged 36 to 45 and increasing by 5% increments for each 5-year period to a maximum of 40% when the contributor is aged 61 or over.

2.9 One interesting strategy for those aged 50 plus is to put £2,808 into a personal pension scheme and take benefits immediately. This will result in an immediate tax-free lump sum of £900, and an annuity based on £2,700, all for a net outlay of just £1,908.

Which route is best?

2.10 Where an individual is in the position that they are able to make contributions to an ISA or a personal pension with no contribution from an employer, but not both, the situation needs to be considered carefully.

2.11 The situation will vary according to an individual's tax position, both at the time they are making payment into an ISA or pension and at the time they want to benefit from the investment.

2.12   Firstly, we will consider a basic rate taxpayer, a male aged 35 making contributions of £200 per month into a pension fund for 25 years until he reaches 60. The contributions gross up to £256 after tax relief, and assuming a growth rate of 7%, and annual management charges of 1%, the fund will grow to £166,000 at age 60. Let us assume that at that point the man either converts the whole sum into an annuity, or alternatively takes 25% as a tax-free lump sum and buys an annuity with the balance.

2.13   The first alternative produces an annual pension, at current annuity rates, of around £11,450, assuming no escalation clause or guarantee or pension to a spouse in the case of death. Assuming the personal allowance and 10% tax band are available, this nets down to £10,177.

2.14   The second alternative produces a lump sum of £41,500, and a pension of around £8,600 on the same basis. This pension nets down to £7,995, using the same assumptions about the personal allowance and tax bands. If we assume an interest rate of 4.5% gross on the lump sum, this produces a further net annual income of £1,457, to give a total net income of £9,411.

2.15   In the case of the first alternative there will be nothing to go into the individual's estate – the pension dies with them and the whole of the lump sum is lost. In the second case, of course, there will be £41,500 available.

2.16   Now let us see what happens if the same £200 per month is invested in an ISA – assuming an ISA or similar vehicle is available for the whole period. Since there is no tax relief, this grows to £129,000 after 25 years, using the same assumptions. The first point to make is that the whole of this £129,000 is available for the individual to do with as they please.

2.17   We will consider three scenarios:

(*a*)   the money is put in a building society account;

(*b*)   £41,500 is put in a building society account and the balance used to buy a purchased life annuity; and

(*c*)   the whole sum is used to buy a purchased life annuity.

In each case we will again assume that the personal allowance and 10% tax band are available, and that the interest on the building society account is 4.5% gross.

2.18   In case (*a*) the net after-tax income will be £5,685. In case (*b*), the combined gross income from the building society account and the annuity is £7,622. Because over £4,000 of the purchased life annuity income is deemed to be return of capital it is not subject to income tax, so the net income is also £7,622. In case (*c*), the income from the annuity is £8,483. Again this will not be subject to tax since almost £6,000 of it is deemed to be return of capital.

2.19   In summary then, we have the following net annual income situation 25 years down the road after saving £200 per month.

(*a*) Via a pension taking no lump sum – available capital
zero   £10,177

(*b*) Via a pension taking 25% lump sum – available capital
£41,500   £9,411

(*c*) Via an ISA, putting proceeds into annuity – available
capital zero   £8,483

(*d*) Via an ISA taking same lump sum as with pension and
putting balance into an annuity – available capital
£41,500   £7,622

(*e*) Via an ISA putting proceeds into building society –
available capital £129,000   £5,685

2.20   This table demonstrates the trade-off between availability of capital and income generated. Also, on the face of it, the pension route is more attractive than the ISA route, unless the investor wants the full proceeds available to use as they will when they reach retirement.

2.21   However, in practice, if one went down the ISA route, one would probably not withdraw the £129,000 from within the tax shelter, rather make withdrawals from it as required, leaving the balance to continue to grow tax-free. These withdrawals will, of course, be totally free of tax.

2.22   Most people going down the pension route will take their 25% lump sum. To achieve the same annual net income of £9,411 by making withdrawals from the ISA requires the ISA fund at retirement (£129,000) to achieve a gross overall annual growth rate of 7.3%, income and capital growth combined, if the fund is not to be eroded. In the long term, for an equity-based investment, this is surely not a wholly unreasonable expectation.

2.23 Remember too that the investor has full access to all the capital whenever they need it, and that capital does not disappear on death, but is available to be bequeathed. Note that, if an individual's estate is liable to IHT, it is not tax-efficient to leave money in an ISA right up to death. An ISA shelters investments from income tax and CGT, but not IHT. On death, as we have seen, IHT supersedes CGT, and the whole of the ISA pot will fall into the estate.

2.24 Ideally, ISAs should be encashed prior to death and the money moved out of the estate – preferably at least seven years before death.

2.25 This example has assumed that we are dealing with a basic rate taxpayer. The sums are exactly the same as above for a higher rate taxpayer who drops to the basic rate on retirement, except that such an individual will receive a further rebate of £554 per year direct, as a reduction in income tax payable to account for the difference between basic and higher rate tax levels.

2.26 Obviously, in this case, the pension route is preferable. If we assume that the £554 per annum is actually saved in an ISA, it will grow to £29,000, on the same assumptions as previously. This is £29,000 that would not, of course, be available if the £200 per month had been put into an ISA instead.

2.27 What about the higher rate taxpayer who remains a higher rate taxpayer on retirement? The following table summarises the net income position, after deduction of tax at 40%, including the effect of the extra £29,000 from the pension alternative, assuming for simplicity that it is withdrawn from the ISA and put in a building society account.

(*a*) Via a pension taking no lump sum – available capital
£29,000   £7,653

(*b*) Via a pension taking 25% lump sum – available capital
£70,500   £7,063

(*c*) Via an ISA, putting proceeds into annuity – available
capital £29,000   £8,267

(*d*) Via an ISA taking same lump sum as with pension and
putting balance into an annuity – available capital
£70,500   £6,980

(*e*) Via an ISA putting proceeds into Building Society –
available capital £158,000   £4,266

2.28   Again, in practice, those who had gone down the ISA route would probably not buy an annuity. To achieve withdrawals the same as from the pension route (£7,063) after taking 25% lump sum, and without diluting the capital, requires annual gross total growth of the ISA funds of 5.5% compared with 7.3% in the previous example. On balance, the ISA route is much more attractive in this second case, requiring a lower annual growth rate of the fund to preserve parity. Furthermore, the net annuity income is virtually the same – £7,063 as against £6,980.

2.29   In summary, it would seem in theory that basic rate taxpayers and higher rate taxpayers who remain on the higher rate in retirement will be better off using the ISA route, all things considered. However, in practice, higher rate taxpayers who can afford to save more than £7,000 per year should put the balance into a pension fund. Remember too, that we are talking about individuals who are either self-employed or do not have access to an employer's scheme to which the employer contributes.

2.30   Finally, those who have no taxable income will always be better off using the pension route, since their contributions up to £2,808 will be grossed up regardless.

Self-invested personal pension

2.31   We turn now to the actual type of pension. In terms of flexibility there is no doubt that a self-invested personal pension (SIPP) is a very attractive option. There are three principal reasons for this. The first is that the investor is able to retain control over how their pension contributions are invested. The second is that there is a wide choice of investment options, and the third is the flexibility when it comes to income drawdown, if applicable.

2.32   SIPPs have been available since the *Finance Act 1989*, and permitted investments include stocks and shares (quoted on the London or a recognised overseas Stock Exchange), unit and investment trusts, insurance company managed funds and unit linked funds, deposit accounts and even commercial property. An investor can choose to put money into any or all of these. Subject only to handling fees, investments can also be moved around within a SIPP without incurring the penalties which are often associated with transferring funds from a standard personal pension plan.

2.33   Benefits are also flexible. A major attraction is that it is possible to dedicate just part of the accumulated funds to income drawdown, whilst leaving the rest to continue to grow. This can have IHT benefits. On death the tax position basically depends upon whether the member has started income drawdown or not. If there has been no income drawdown the fund can be distributed in most circumstances to the chosen beneficiaries free of IHT.

2.34   Once income drawdown has started there is a special tax charge of 35% on that element of the fund only. Spouses can take pension from the fund after the member's death and can then nominate further beneficiaries to receive the remaining lump sum. Of course, this flexibility terminates at 75, when an annuity must be purchased.

2.35   Furthermore, using a SIPP, an investor with their own business can benefit that business through the purchase of a suitable commercial property in the UK to be used in connection with it. The business leases the premises from the pension trustees at a full commercial rent as confirmed by a qualified valuer.

2.36   High earning individuals about to retire from a company which has an occupational pension scheme should also consider a SIPP. Someone earning £100,000 a year and retiring at 60 might expect a lump sum of £150,000 and an annual index-linked pension of £50,000 a year. If they pre-decease their spouse, the spouse might expect £25,000 per year for life. After that there is no pay-out to anyone else.

2.37   However, before any benefits are taken, there is the opportunity to transfer to a SIPP. The transfer value might be of the order of £1million and the same lump sum can be taken. The balance of the money can be invested according to the needs of the individual concerned. Often there may be sufficient money from cashing share options or consultancy or part-time directorships to provide an income without touching the fund. Again, on death the tax position basically depends upon whether the member has started income drawdown or not. It is always sensible to ask a firm of pension consultants to carry out a transfer value analysis when contemplating this route. The fee – typically £1,500 – will be well spent.

2.38   As to other fees a client will incur with a SIPP, there is usually a set-up charge which can vary from £250 up to £800 and an annual charge, usually fixed, which can typically vary from £225 up to £750. In addition to this each transaction will generate a charge which tends to vary between £15 and £30.

2.39   There are two main alternative ways to set up a SIPP. The first involves using specialised pension managers, while the second is via one of the traditional insurance companies using a hybrid scheme. Here an investor usually has to make certain minimum contributions to the insurance company's in-house pension scheme and can then have access to a SIPP. The SIPP element is often administered by one of the specialist pension managers. One possible advantage of this method is that the insurance company will often have negotiated favourable charging rates for dealing with the SIPP.

Small self-administered scheme

2.40   If a client is working in a business which currently has no occupational pension scheme, they might well consider a small self-administered scheme (SSAS). This is essentially an occupational scheme limited to a maximum of eleven people within the same company. However, the rules are not as exacting as a normal occupational scheme. Generally speaking a SSAS is exempt from the *Pensions Act 1995* and the Occupational Pensions Regulatory Authority.

2.41   One major advantage of a SSAS is that it allows a business owner to utilise the SSAS funds for the benefit of the company. The following table sets out a summary of all the main differences between a SSAS and a SIPP.

	SSAS	SIPP
Trustees	Usually all members are trustees plus a Pensioneer Trustee	Individual arrangement may be set up under Deed Poll or under trust with member as co-trustee.
Investment decisions	Usually unanimous decision of all trustees as evidenced in writing.	Individual choice.
Investment options	Quoted investments Commercial property Unquoted investments Loans Self-investment	Unit trusts/pooled funds (FSA recognised or overseas regulated) Quoted investments Commercial property (if purchased from unconnected party)
Borrowing	Limits depending on value of fund and contributions paid.	75% of purchase price of property asset being purchased.
Maximum benefits	Dependent upon earnings and service. For members with pre-1989 rights no restriction on earnings that can be pensioned.	Whatever pension is purchased by fund at retirement.

	SSAS	SIPP	
Maximum contributions	As advised by Actuary to meet maximum benefits.	Age	% of earnings
		Up to 35	17.5%
		36–45	20.0%
		46–50	25.0%
		51–55	30.0%
		56–60	35.0%
		61–74	40.0%
		earnings subject to CAP (currently £97,200)	
Death benefits before retirement	Maximum benefits based on salary and service. Lump sum of up to four times salary to dependants. Spouse's pension of up to 4/9ths of salary depending on potential service. Excess assets returned to company subject to tax.	Fund in respect of contributions paid out as lump sum to dependants. Up to ¼ of fund in respect of transfers in from occupational schemes may be paid as lump sum to dependants. Balance of fund used to provide spouse's pension. If no spouse, or transfer not originally from occupational scheme, balance paid as lump sum. If separate life insurance, total lump sum benefits restricted to 4 times salary including SIPP benefits, or 2 times salary excluding SIPP benefits.	
Retirement	Any age 50–75. Must actually retire unless member has continued rights, when they can take benefits at NRD and continue working.	Any age 50–75. Can take benefits and continue working.	
Income Flexibility	Can choose income between levels advised by Actuary. Can alternatively use drawdown flexibility if SSAS rules permit	Flexibility to move income levels up and down within specified ranges.	
Tax-free cash	Based on service and salary. Can only take once.	¼ of fund. Occasional limits on tax-free cash from any transfers in from occupational scheme. May be able to take cash over period of time.	

Source: Suffolk Life – based on understanding and interpretation of current law and Inland Revenue practice.

Income drawdown

2.42 Finally, before we leave the topic of pensions, how do you decide if a client is best taking income drawdown or not? Income drawdown investments are suitable for:

- Individuals with reasonably substantial funds of at least £250,000 and who are not averse to risk.

- Individuals wishing to take advantage of receiving their tax-free cash immediately and requiring some income, whilst delaying the purchase of their annuity.

- Individuals who believe that they can invest to produce a greater return during their retirement than they could achieve with the immediate purchase of a standard annuity.

- Individuals going into semi-retirement who require some initial income but who want the opportunity to invest their pension fund until they retire completely.

- Individuals who wish to protect the majority of their pension fund for their family should they die before the age of 75. Unlike an annuity, with income drawdown, a lump sum, less tax, can be payable if the fundholder dies before age 75.

- Individuals already investing in a self-invested personal pension (SIPP) and who would like to continue to be involved in investment decisions, since income drawdown is a natural extension of a SIPP.

- Individuals with younger spouses wishing to preserve their pension fund whilst maintaining investment flexibility.

- Individuals retiring at 50, or soon after, who feel that they could benefit more by purchasing an annuity when they are older. The older you become the more attractive a standard annuity becomes when compared to the annuity rate for a healthy younger person, which will be lower.

- Individuals requiring income flexibility to deal with expenses or windfalls. For example, the marriage expenses of a child or grandchild might necessitate a higher income requirement in one year than they would normally require. Alternatively, those retirees who have other investments maturing in various tax years might want to reduce their taxable income from their income drawdown during these years.

- Individuals with substantial funds requiring part of their fund to provide a minimum guaranteed income whilst the balance provides the potential of higher returns in their later years.

- Individuals with below average health who may wish to maximise the benefits on death to their spouse or dependants if they feel this could occur before the age of 75. It should be noted, however, that the Capital Taxes Office has indicated that they would be concerned if a terminally ill person with a very short life expectancy took income drawdown.

2.43   Those who would not benefit from drawdown include:

- Individuals who have a cautious attitude to investment risk, who will probably prefer the complete peace of mind that is given by a standard annuity which provides a guaranteed income for life.

- Individuals with smaller funds which could quickly be eroded by administration costs and ongoing charges. There is also the potential risk that as a result of poor investment performance they would be worse off than if they had purchased a standard annuity at outset.

- Individuals who do not wish to be involved with regularly monitoring their investments.

- Individuals who require the maximum possible income without the necessary increase in investment risk.

2.44   Clients may only take tax-free cash when they first take income drawdown. If they do not, then they are no longer entitled to it, and it remains invested in the pension fund. If cash has been transferred from a company pension scheme, the amount of tax-free cash may be restricted by Inland Revenue limits.

2.45   The amount of income that can be withdrawn varies within limits. These limits are set by the Government Actuary and are related to current top annuity rates.

2.46   The maximum income is similar to the income which would be provided by a standard single life, level annuity with no guarantee, payable monthly in arrears. The minimum is 35% of that figure. Under the current rules, the Government Actuary imposes a review of these limits for each individual plan every three years. As the income limits are directly linked to annuity rates, they increase with age. This often means that the amount which can be drawn down will increase at the triennial review.

Offset mortgages

2.47   Another tax-efficient ploy for those clients who have a mortgage on their house is an offset arrangement. Lenders are increasingly offering this facility, and it is particularly attractive for the higher rate taxpayer.

2.48   The principle of offset is deceptively straightforward. Clients simply take out a mortgage in the usual way – either interest only or repayment. In conjunction with this they also open a separate savings account. Now comes the clever bit! They are not paid any interest on their savings. Instead, the amount of interest paid on the loan is reduced, that is, offset against the savings. Calculations are done daily, so any alteration in the savings account is instantly reflected in the amount of interest charged on the loan.

2.49   A good way of looking at the offset savings account is to consider it as a cash ISA, with three extra advantages. Firstly, you can only put £3,000 into an actual cash ISA, whereas if you have an £80,000 mortgage, you can effectively have an £80,000 tax-sheltered investment. Secondly, if you withdraw, say, £2,000 from this year's cash ISA, you cannot top it up again during the current tax year. There is no such restriction with offset. Thirdly, the rate of return is better!

2.50   So, for example if a client has a mortgage of £80,000 on the one hand, and £10,000 in their savings account on the other, they will pay interest on just £70,000. Say the mortgage rate is 5%. This means that clients are effectively receiving 5% on their savings.

2.51   However, because they have not been credited with any interest, there is no tax to pay on it. This means that the notional 5% received on the savings is actually a net return. This is equivalent to 6.25% gross for a basic rate taxpayer, and 8.3% for a higher rate taxpayer.

2.52   The beauty of an offset mortgage arrangement is that it is so uncomplicated. Although the accounts are linked together for interest calculation purposes, they are totally separate. Clients can operate each entirely independently of the other, and in particular pay in or draw out as much as they want from their savings account at any time.

2.53   The amount that can be offset is only limited by the outstanding amount of the mortgage. Those with an interest-only loan can build up a lump sum to repay it, secure in the knowledge that they are getting a good rate of interest with total security of capital.

Investing in property

2.54   Property investments should also be considered seriously. Investing in buy-to-let properties is increasingly viewed as an alternative to more traditional savings vehicles. A major attraction is that property is an easy investment to understand. Further, it does not have the unpredictability of being dependent upon the ups and downs of the stock market.

2.55   Furthermore, investment properties can be seen as a long-term opportunity to replace a pension. This gives control over the assets which is not available if the money is tied up in a pension fund. Upon death, the asset passes to the estate and the value can be realised prior to retirement if required. These options are not usually available with a pension.

2.56   Firstly, let us consider residential buy-to-let. Location of the property is of prime importance. Things to consider include closeness to local amenities or major employers. The right location will ensure a better chance of maintaining constant demand and achieving high capital growth. The most popular type of property seems to be one- or two-bedroom flats. These need to be of a high quality to attract the right calibre of tenant and to generate the right yield.

2.57   It is important to check whether there are any service charges on the property. In the case of leasehold properties, there will normally also be a ground rent to be considered. Maintenance costs and insurance premiums must all be taken into account.

2.58   If the property is to be let furnished, all furnishings must comply with rigorous safety standards and the cost of this must be accommodated for. A prudent investor will also allow in their calculations for any likely period when the property is not let and therefore producing no income.

2.59   Recent *Investors Chronicle* figures indicate that the annual return on a £200,000 house, after meeting all expenses, including a 15% letting agent's fee so that the investor has no concerns about finding or renting a property, collecting the rent or paying the outgoings, can be 7% before tax. Furthermore, some capital appreciation is to be expected in the medium to long term.

2.60   If clients intend to gear up their investment via a mortgage, they should calculate the cash flow implications very carefully. They should consider the worse case scenario in which interest rates rise, rental yields fall and the property suffers a letting void, and ensure that they do not over-borrow and leave themselves vulnerable to a negative cash flow situation and a possible forced sale.

2.61 We turn now to commercial buy-to-let. There is less hassle finding tenants for commercial property since leases run for up to 25 years, compared with 2 to 3 on the residential front, and sometimes as little as 6 months. Again, the income stream from a good commercial tenant on a long lease makes it relatively easy to persuade a lender to provide a mortgage. On the repairs and insurance front, the residential landlord is often responsible. This contrasts with a commercial lease where there is usually a fully repairing and insuring clause, placing these costs on the tenant.

2.62 What about the returns? These will mainly depend upon the length of the unexpired portion of the lease, and the quality of the tenant – that is the strength of the covenant. A property which has a good tenant on a long lease will show 7–7.5% before agent's fees, rising to 10% if the tenant and the quality of the covenant are not so good.

2.63 What about finance? Commercial mortgages are a more specialised market than residential, and off-the-shelf products are not usually available. Each loan will be negotiated according to the particular circumstances of the proposition.

2.64 The three most important elements are the quality of the property, the status of the tenant and the status of the borrower. The first two are self-explanatory. The status of the borrower is a key factor in case a tenant is late with the rent payments or defaults. A prospective lender likes to be reassured that a borrower is not solely reliant on the rental income to fund the loan. Quality of location also matters as this will impact on the vacancy period once the lease has expired, and also on the rent achievable.

2.65 Depending upon these criteria, a loan can be arranged for up to 75% of the property's value at a rate of interest varying from 1.5% over London Inter Bank Offer Rate (LIBOR) to 4% over. The rate of interest is usually fixed for three months, and then readjusted to reflect the current LIBOR.

2.66 Where do you go to find commercial property to buy? The three main sources are commercial auctions, local commercial agents who know the patch well or specialised investment teams that cater for the small investor.

2.67 Rental income is taxed under Schedule A in the year in which it arises less any allowable expenses – maintenance, agent's fees, loan interest and the like. Standard rate taxpayers will pay 22%, and higher rate taxpayers 40%. Any capital gain will be subject to CGT and the property asset is a non-business one for the purposes of taper relief.

Single premium bonds

2.68 Single premium bonds can be tax efficient, particularly for higher rate taxpayers who expect to become basic rate taxpayers at a later date. There is no tax charge on withdrawals from the bond for a basic rate taxpayer. However, care must be taken that withdrawals or encashment of the bond will not affect an individual's claim to full age allowance, if appropriate. The savings income arising on the underlying investment of the bond within the life company's fund is taxed at 20%. Capital gains arising are taxed at 20% unless the bond is linked solely to government securities, in which case no charges to CGT arise. There is no annual CGT exemption in the bond.

2.69 Higher rate taxpayers can defer the charge to higher rate income tax for 20 years if they withdraw no more than 5% each premium year of their original investment. The unused annual 5% cumulative allowances can be carried forward and used in later years. For example, if no withdrawals are made in years one to four, in year five up to 25% of the original lump sum could be withdrawn without a charge to income tax arising at that stage.

2.70 Withdrawals in excess of 5% per annum are subjected to the difference between the higher rate tax and the basic rate tax credit, even when there has been no capital gain or, indeed, when there has actually been a loss. The procedure is followed on the eventual withdrawal of 100% of the original premium, total encashment of the bond, the death of the life assured or the assignment of the policy for money's worth.

2.71 When the bond is cashed in, top slicing relief is available. The gain for income tax purposes will be calculated in the following way.

2.72 The cash value of the bond, plus any previous withdrawals and partial encashments, minus the client's total investment in the bond, minus any previous chargeable gains, equals the gain for income tax purposes.

2.73 A gain for income tax purposes may arise on distribution, on a full or partial surrender, or on death. The gain from the bond will be added to the client's income for the relevant year. If the client is a higher rate taxpayer, or if the gain added to their income makes them a higher rate taxpayer, they will be liable to pay the difference between the basic rate and higher rate of income tax on the gain.

2.74   The amount of tax paid on the gain can be reduced by top slicing. This is where the client's gain is divided by the number of complete years they have held their bond, even if part of their total investment was made at a later date. This gives the average yearly gain – the slice – which is then added to the client's income in the year of the encashment. This determines what tax rate they should pay. If they are within the basic rate tax band no additional income tax is due. If the slice takes them into the higher rate band then the difference between higher rate and basic rate income tax is due on the amount of the slice above the higher rate threshold.

2.75   The amount of tax due from this calculation is then multiplied by the number of complete years the bond has been held to give the total amount of tax due. Top slicing can mean that if a client fully cashes in their bond at a time when their income is lower, say after retirement, they can minimise any tax liability.

National savings and investment products

2.76   One final thought for higher rate taxpayers is Savings Certificates and Premium Bonds. Up to £10,000 can be invested in each issue of five-year Fixed Interest Savings Certificates. The current issue – the sixty-third – pays 3.45%. Since this is tax-free it equates to 5.75% gross for a higher rate taxpayer. Prizes on Premium Bonds are also free of tax, and they range from £50 up to £1million. At the current odds, someone who invested the maximum £20,000 and enjoyed average luck, could expect to receive eight tax-free prizes a year.

2.77   If these were all £50 minimum, the gross annual return equates to 3.3%, through 3.75% if just one of the eight was £100, up to a respectable 5% if four were £100. The major attraction is, of course, the slim possibility of picking up one of the larger prizes.

Married couples

2.78   Couples should ensure that both of them take full advantage of their personal allowances and lower and basic rate tax bands. If one of a couple has no income, then investments and savings other than shares should be put in their name to utilise these.

2.79   It is also worthwhile transferring shares from one to the other, if the transferor is a higher rate taxpayer and the other a basic rate taxpayer. This avoids the extra tax charge on the dividend which would otherwise be payable. In the case of a married couple chargeable assets can be transferred from one to the other without triggering a CGT charge.

2.80   The spouse taking over the assets is deemed to have acquired them at the same time and at the same price as the transferor. Any transfer must be an outright gift and there should be proper written evidence of it – a letter from one to the other, signed and dated, will suffice. There is no stamp duty on gifts.

2.81   As far as jointly owned assets are concerned, spouses are normally deemed to own such property as joint tenants. This means that each owns 50%, and when one dies their share automatically passes to the other. It is also possible to hold joint assets as tenants in common. In this case each spouse's share is separate and may be unequal. Further, the share may be disposed of in lifetime or on death, exactly as each spouse wishes, rather than passing to the other. There must be proper documentary evidence to show that a tenancy in common exists.

2.82   This can be a particularly useful device where the richer of two spouses does not want to make a significant transfer of assets to the other. A tenancy in common can be created whereby one spouse owns 99% of the asset and the other 1%. Since the couple is married, tax law deems that any income arising on the jointly held asset is divided equally between them, provided that no declaration has been made to the contrary.

Product opportunities

- ISAs
- Personal Pension Plans
- SIPPs
- SSAS
- National Savings
- Immediate Vesting Annuities
- Offset Mortgages
- Buy-to-Let Mortgages
- Commercial Mortgages
- Single Premium Bonds

Chapter 3

Basic Mitigation of CGT

The annual exemption

3.1   The first thing is for a taxpayer to ensure that they utilise their annual exempt allowance each year. This can be done by a simple sale of shares, which must not be bought back again in less than 31 days or the transaction will be invalid for CGT purposes.

3.2   If there are allowable losses, we have already seen that these can be set against chargeable gains in an order that gives the taxpayer the greatest benefit from taper relief and thus results in the lowest amount chargeable to CGT. In other words, losses should first be set against gains which qualify for the least taper relief.

3.3   Allowable losses realised in the current tax year must be set against gains, even if this reduces them below the amount of the exemption (£7,700). Losses brought forward need only be utilised to reduce the net gain, before taper relief, to the amount of the exemption. The balance of any losses can be carried forward.

3.4   Losses need careful management, particularly since, as time goes on, the level of taper relief for non-business assets rises to 40%. Being forced to use losses to reduce gains down to the level of or below the exempt amount means that taper relief, which is unlimited, is being foregone at the expense of losses, which are finite.

3.5   There are ways to utilise the annual exempt allowance without disrupting the portfolio. Husband and wife couples can swap holdings. This must be done through the stock exchange. Each sells shares to utilise their exempt allowance and the other purchases corresponding shares on the same day. If such couples hold shares jointly, they can separate their portfolios by gifting shares to each other first.

3.6   As previously mentioned there are no CGT implications at the time of the gift – the shares simply pass from one to the other at their original cost and purchase date. Another simple strategy is to transfer shares into a self-select ISA. The transfer will be deemed to take place at market value and any chargeable gain to that date can be set off against the annual exempt amount.

3.7   Gifting holdings can also be used to reduce the level of CGT payable. If one spouse is not utilising their starting or basic rate tax bands, a gift before sale may be advantageous.

3.8   Care should be taken to ensure that the Inland Revenue cannot contend that in reality, despite any formalities, there was no effective transfer. For example, if an asset transferred is sold shortly afterwards and the proceeds go only to the transferor spouse, could the Revenue contend there was an agreement, or understanding thereon when the transfer took place? It would be preferable if the proceeds went only to an account of the transferee spouse or at the very least to an account in joint names.

3.9   If an agreement or understanding has been reached with a third party for disposal of the asset before the inter-spouse transfer, this may well provoke the Inland Revenue into contending that the inter-spouse transfer should be ignored on the application of the *Ramsay* and *Furniss v Dawson* principles (case law principles which can counteract tax avoidance schemes in certain circumstances). Prudently, the inter-spouse transfer should take place prior thereto.

Furnished holiday lettings

3.10   There is one particular property investment – furnished holiday lettings – which is classed as a business asset. This means that any capital gain is subject to business taper relief, which reduces the effective rate of CGT for a higher rate taxpayer to just 20% once the property has been held for 12 months and 10% once it has been held for two years or more. The corresponding effective rates for a basic rate taxpayer are 10% and 5%.

3.11   Furnished holiday lettings are a special type of letting to encourage the holding of property in leisure areas. There are some special conditions to be met:

- the property must be in the UK;
- it must be available for letting to the public for at least 140 days per year;
- it must actually be let for at least 70 days per year;
- it must not be occupied by the same person for a continuous period exceeding 31 days.

3.12 If investors require a mortgage it will be subject to the normal buy-to-let rules. Since, on a holiday let, the rental income will not flow in evenly, the total expected annual income will be divided by 12 to give the average monthly amount to which the repayments are geared.

3.13 Any mortgage application must usually be accompanied by a written report from an independent letting agent, either giving a two-year history of the property's letting record, or an estimate of expected rental income. The borrower's income does not normally enter into the calculation, subject to it being a minimum of £10,000 per year.

3.14 There are some other tax advantages arising from the fact that furnished holiday lettings are treated as a trade. Any income received qualifies as relevant earnings with respect to contributions into a personal pension plan. Furthermore, if a furnished holiday letting property is sold, and the proceeds used to purchase another one within the next three years, a claim can be made for any chargeable gain on the one sold to be deferred.

3.15 Alternatively, if an additional property has been bought in the 12 months prior to disposal, any chargeable gain can again be deferred back. Again, if a chargeable gain has been realised on other business assets, this gain can itself be deferred by investment in a furnished holiday letting.

3.16 Anyone aged 50 or over, or retiring earlier because of ill-health, can claim retirement relief on any chargeable gain when a furnished holiday letting is sold. There is 100% relief on gains up to £50,000 and 50% relief on the excess up to maximum gains of £200,000. From 2003–04 onwards this relief is not available.

CGT-free investments

3.17 What about investments that are CGT-free? Two securities which fall into this category are government loan stock – gilts – and building society permanent interest-bearing shares (PIBS).

Gilts

3.18 Like any individual the Government has to balance its income and expenditure. When short-term expenditure exceeds income, the Treasury meets this shortfall by borrowing money – issuing gilts.

3.19 These can be bought or sold through the stock exchange, using a stockbroker, or direct from the Bank of England Brokerage Service, using an application form from the local Post Office. Current prices are listed daily in good quality newspapers alongside share prices or, in the case of the *Financial Times*, on a separate page devoted to capital markets.

3.20 The most common name is Treasury, but Exchequer and Consolidated also crop up. These names derive from the government department raising the money or the use to which it was to be put, but now have no particular significance. Most gilts have a set repayment date and stocks are listed in order of repayment. Some six stocks are undated, and are repayable entirely at the government's discretion.

3.21 How do we interpret the *FT* gilt tables? Let us look at typical stock, say, Treasury 9% 2008. This means that when the stock was issued, the government was prepared to pay 9% interest, and the loan will be repaid in 2008 at issue price, known as par. The first two columns give yield figures and the third column the current price for each £100 worth of stock. Let us say these figures are 7.28% and 5.34% and £123.57 respectively. The current price is a mid-market price and there will be a spread of around 6p on the price to buy and the price to sell. The first yield figure is the running yield. This is the return an investor will get at the current price. Each £100 worth of stock generates £9 interest each year and this represents an actual return of 7.28% on the current price.

3.22 The important figure an investor should consider is the second one, which shows the gross redemption yield (GRY). This takes account of the fact that if you buy today and hold the stock until redemption you will lose nearly £24 of your capital. When this is spread over the remaining life of the gilt, it reduces the effective yield – the GRY – down to 5.34%.

3.23 Interest is paid twice a year gross and stock is normally sold with it accumulated. The letters 'xd' appear after the price seven days before interest is paid. This means that it does not go to the buyer, but is paid to the seller. The final three columns in the tables show daily price movements and yearly high and low figures for the stock.

3.24 Index-linked gilts are slightly different in that both the interest paid and the redemption value are linked to inflation as measured by the retail price index.

3.25 Gilt strips are a newcomer to the scene, introduced in late 1997. A strip separates a bond into its component parts, one for each interest payment, known as a coupon strip, and one that receives the repayment value, a principal strip. The attraction is that a strip delivers certainty. In the case of a principal strip, for example, the investor buys it at a discount to the face value and is guaranteed to receive face value when it matures.

3.26 Two main factors will cause gilt prices to move. The first is interest rates. This means both short-term rates, now set by the Bank of England's monetary policy committee, and long-term rates, set by investors' willingness to lend to the government over, say, 5, 10 or 15 years. Long-term interest rates are very sensitive to forecasts of future inflation.

3.27 To take a simple example, if the government issued stock at a time when the prevailing rate was 12%, that is what they would have to pay to be competitive and that rate is fixed for the life of the gilt. Suppose that five years later prevailing interest rates have dropped to 6%. The market price of the stock will have doubled, all other things being equal, to reflect the lower interest rate. Similarly if interest rates rise, the price of gilts will drop.

3.28 The second important factor is supply and demand. If there are more willing buyers than sellers, prices will move up, and vice versa. There has been relatively little government borrowing required of late. This factor, combined with the fact that pension funds are major buyers of gilts, has tended to increase gilt prices, and therefore depress yields.

3.29 Regarding taxation, income received is subject to income tax at the holder's marginal rate. On ordinary gilts any capital gains are free of CGT for individual investors. In the case of gilt strips all profits are assessable each year as income, with no charge to CGT. Any loss can be deducted from other taxable income for the year.

Permanent interest-bearing shares

3.30 We turn now to PIBS. Building societies can raise additional capital by issuing PIBS. These are similar to corporate bonds because they pay a fixed rate of interest. However, they have no redemption date.

3.31 Interest is paid twice a year net of basic rate tax. It is not possible, as it is with building society interest, for a non-taxpayer to elect to receive the interest gross, but they can reclaim the tax deducted. A higher rate taxpayer will have to pay a further 20% tax. If PIBS are sold at a profit, the gain is not liable to capital gains tax. PIBS can be included in the stocks and shares component of an ISA.

3.32 Although PIBS were originally aimed at institutional investors, they were quickly recycled into the hands of private investors. This was because of the attractive yields, the freedom from capital gains tax and the fact that PIBS confer membership rights on their holders. On demutualisation, therefore, PIBS holders are entitled to a share in any windfall profits.

3.33 No UK stamp duty is payable on the issue or transfer of PIBS. They are traded on the stock exchange and can be bought and sold through a stockbroker who will charge commission in the same way as for gilts. The price of PIBS tends to move in tandem with long gilts – those with over 15 years to run. Although PIBS prices track long gilts, they give a higher yield, typically some 2.25% higher.

3.34 The market in PIBS is relatively small so the shares are not always easy to buy and sell. They are therefore not a good investment for people who need quick access to their savings. They are also unsuitable for those who need absolute security of capital. For an ordinary building society savings account, the deposit protection scheme gives up to £18,000 protection of capital if the society gets into trouble. There is no such protection with PIBS, and if a building society has to be wound up, PIBS shareholders are the last to receive any money. Current prices are shown in the *FT Money* section each Saturday.

Traded endowment policies

3.35 Another investment on which any profits are subject to CGT rather than income tax is traded endowment policies (TEPs), as long as the policies are qualifying ones. Essentially, qualifying policies are whole-life and endowments with terms of ten or more years.

3.36 TEPs are traditional with-profit policies with a guaranteed sum assured and attaching annual and terminal bonuses. When purchased, the guaranteed sum assured together with the annual bonuses paid thus far is guaranteed. Future annual bonuses and terminal bonuses are, of course, not guaranteed. Estimates of the likely final return are provided by market makers, based on previous history, prevailing market conditions and expectations of future market conditions.

3.37 An investor in a TEP pays a capital sum together with the agreement to pay all future premiums until the policy matures. They will then be entitled to the maturity proceeds. Maturity will be at a fixed future date, or earlier if the person who took out the policy dies. TEPs are subject to CGT with the gain calculated as maturity proceeds less purchase price together with premiums paid. The CGT is assessed in the same way as it is for other assets. Qualifying policies can be transferred between spouses without charge to CGT. This will be relevant if one spouse has not used their annual exempt allowance or is in a lower tax bracket than the other.

Other basic strategies

3.38 CGT is due on 31 January following the end of the tax year. So for a sale in the year to 5 April 2003, any tax is due on 31 January 2004. Postponing the sale by one day to 6 April means that any tax will not be due until 31 January 2005. However, this is not the only consideration, since deferring a sale may result in a taxpayer forfeiting their annual exempt amount. This cannot be carried forward or back and is lost forever if not used each year. Further, a basic rate taxpayer needs to consider whether or not the gain will push them into the higher rate tax bracket for a particular year.

3.39 A parent can gift shares to children under 18. Any income arising in excess of £100 will be treated as the parent's, but any capital gain will be the child's and subject to the child's own annual exempt allowance.

3.40 Another way to utilise the annual exempt allowance is to buy zero dividend shares in carefully selected split capital investment trusts, which are not mainly invested in other split trusts. An astute investor can buy a series of zeros to mature in years when they do not anticipate fully utilising their allowance. The process can be fine-tuned, because the shares can be sold through the stock market at any time before maturity.

Product opportunities

- Zero Dividend Investment Trust Shares
- Buy-to-Let Mortgages
- Gilts
- PIBs
- TEPs

Chapter 4

Basic Mitigation of IHT

Wills

4.1   A will can be a very useful tool in IHT planning. The Law Society estimates that two out of three people die without having made a will, that is intestate. In these circumstances there is a set of intestacy rules to determine how the estate is divided. If there is a spouse and no other surviving relatives then the whole estate passes to them. However, a spouse will not inherit under the intestacy rules if they die within 28 days of the first death.

4.2   If the estate is substantial and there are children or grandchildren, a spouse will finish up with just £125,000 and a life-interest in half of the remainder of the estate. If there are no children the spouse will get the first £200,000 and again, a life-interest in half of the remainder. The balance will go to the parents of the deceased, or brothers and sisters or nephews and nieces.

4.3   It is obviously best to make a will. Firstly, it simplifies the task of determining exactly who has what and secondly it makes the affairs of the deceased easier to deal with. It will be assumed that a solicitor is used to draw up the will, however, clients will be well advised to consider the following.

4.4   It is essential that the will is properly made. It must be signed by the testator and witnessed by two individuals. These must be present at the same time. The witnesses or their spouses must not benefit under the will.

4.5   The testator must be 18 or over and of sound mind when they make the will. They should understand the nature and effect of it. If there is any doubt, medical evidence should be obtained at the time it is drawn up. The testator must not make the will, or part of it, as a result of force, fear, fraud or pressure from another person.

4.6 The language of the will must be clear so that its interpretation is not open to doubt. Otherwise there might be conflict after the death of the testator, or the will might be invalid.

4.7 Certain people are entitled under the law to share in the estate. These include a spouse and anyone financially dependent on the deceased. They should be considered at the drafting stage so that conflicts can be avoided later. Alternatively, trustees can be given discretion so that they are in a position to negotiate if there is a dispute.

4.8 When choosing an executor most people opt for their spouse or children. Permission should always be obtained before appointing executors, since problems can arise if someone declines to deal with an estate. Unlike witnesses, executors can be beneficiaries. Indeed, it may be advisable to make a small bequest to an executor since they are only allowed to claim out-of-pocket expenses from the estate and nothing for their time.

4.9 Professional executors – solicitors, accountants or bank managers – are allowed to charge fees for their time and their scale of charges should be checked carefully before they are appointed. The Public Trustee can be appointed as executor and this may be appropriate if there is no one able and willing to act or where a beneficiary is an incapacitated adult or a dependent child likely to outlive both parents and other close relatives.

4.10 Marriage or re-marriage makes a will invalid unless it was made in contemplation of marriage Therefore a will should usually be revised on marriage. Divorce does not automatically invalidate a will. Minor changes can be made to an existing will by means of a codicil – a supplement to a will. Any codicil must be correctly witnessed, but the witnesses do not need to be the same as for the original will. For substantial changes a new will should be made revoking the former one. The original document should never be altered.

Basic planning

4.11 It will be obvious from the introductory explanation about how IHT operates that the simplest form of planning is to give away as much as possible. Obviously, the simplest way to avoid IHT is to give away one's assets prior to death! It is not just as straightforward as that, since transfers out of an estate in the years prior to death can, in certain circumstances, still be brought into account.

4.12   However, many gifts made during a lifetime are completely exempt from tax, and the principal ones are as follows:

- The first £3,000 of lifetime transfers in any tax year are exempt. Any unused portion of the exemption may be carried forward for one year only for use in the following tax year after the exemption for that following tax year has been used.

- Gifts in consideration of marriage of up to £5,000 by a parent, £2,500 by a grandparent, £2,500 by one party to the marriage to the other, or £1,000 by anyone else.

- Normal expenditure out of income. To obtain exemption the gift must be part of normal expenditure, and must not, taking one year with another, reduce available net income (after all other transfers) below that required to maintain the individuals usual standard of living. Their exemption will often apply to life assurance policy premiums paid for the benefit of someone else.

- A waiver or repayment of remuneration does not attract IHT. Nor does a waiver of dividends made within twelve months before any right to the dividend arises.

- Individuals may sometimes need to make transfers of capital in order to provide for their family, for example, following divorce. Such transfers are exempt.

- Transfers between husband and wife. These are also exempt if they occur at death, either through a will or an intestacy. These are not necessarily tax-efficient (see below).

4.13   Apart from these exempt transfers, most other transfers are potentially exempt – that is they will only be subject to tax if the individual dies within seven years of making them. Essentially, all outright gifts fall into this category. However, property given away is still treated as belonging to the donor for IHT purposes if the donor continues to enjoy any benefit from it – this is known as reservation of benefit.

4.14   The other class of transfers out of an estate are known as chargeable lifetime transfers. The main example of these are transfers to a discretionary trust – one in which no one has a right to the income, and it is up to the trustees how much of the income, if any, they distribute. Chargeable lifetime transfers are immediately chargeable to IHT at the reduced rate of 20%. However, the nil rate band of £250,000 is available, to the extent that it has not already been used against earlier chargeable transfers. The annual £3,000 exemption is also available.

4.15 Discretionary trusts are particularly useful when a client wants to remove assets from their estate, but not give absolute control of them, or the right to income from them, to someone else. A new nil rate band becomes available every seven years. At the current rate this gives the opportunity to make repeated transfers of £250,000 into trust, without incurring any immediate IHT liability. The seriously wealthy can make transfers in excess of £250,000, and as long as they survive for seven years, the rate of IHT payable is just 20% rather than 40%, although it has to be paid at the time of transfer.

4.16 Discretionary trusts are liable to income tax on their income. The general rate payable is 34%. UK dividend income, however, is charged at 25%. Since there has already been a 10% deduction at source, a further 16.7% of the net is due. Payments of income to beneficiaries will be net of income tax at 34%, and they can reclaim it if their income is less than available personal allowances. Note that if payments of income or capital are paid to unmarried children aged under 18 of the settlor, these payments will be deemed to be income of the settlor.

4.17 From April 1999, if a discretionary trust has operated a policy of full distribution of income, higher rate taxpaying beneficiaries receiving dividends on shares through the trust could be up to 12% worse off than if they received the same dividends directly. It must be stressed that there is no problem if the trust's income is interest rather than dividends, nor if beneficiaries are non-taxpayers. Trusts that are fully distributed and invested in equities, could consider making payments to taxpaying beneficiaries out of capital rather than out of income.

4.18 On the CGT front, any capital gains on the transfer of chargeable assets into a trust can be held over until realised by the trustees. Similarly if these same assets are transferred out of trust to a beneficiary, an election for hold-over relief can again be made. Any chargeable gains which arise in the trust are taxable at 34% although the trust has an annual exemption of £3,850. When considering which assets to transfer into a trust, it may be better to select those with little or no CGT liability. This is because assets which are retained in the estate avoid CGT on death.

4.19 Every ten years discretionary trusts are subject to a periodic charge. However, this will never amount to more than 6%, and will often be less. This is because the trust effectively inherits the settlor's nil rate band. If this has not been used, and assets of, say, £250,000 are transferred in, they can grow by a further £250,000 before there is any liability to the periodic charge. Even then it will only be 6% on the excess.

4.20 Shares in a family company can be put into a discretionary trust to utilise Business Property Relief. This gives exemption without limit from IHT either on lifetime transfer or on death. Using a trust means that those transferring the shares can retain control of them until the next generation is mature enough to take over. The only proviso is that the person gifting the shares and their spouse are excluded from benefit.

4.21 A brief mention should be made of what has become known as the 'cascade' effect. This involves a series of small discretionary trusts set up in fairly close proximity by the same settlor. Assuming the settlor has made no chargeable transfers within the previous seven years he can, for example, effect ten settlements each holding £25,000 so that the aggregate equates to the 2002–03 nil rate band of £250,000. Provided the appreciation within each discretionary trust, when aggregated to the initial value of each previous discretionary trust made within the previous seven years, never exceeds £250,000, then no charge to IHT could arise either on the ten-year basis or on exit.

4.22 By way of example, a settlor effects five discretionary settlements in fairly close proximity and transfers £25,000 to each. In the case of the fifth settlement effected, provided that the current value of its trust fund never exceeds £150,000 (i.e. £250,000 – 4 × £25,000), no IHT will ever become payable in connection therewith. Widening this concept somewhat, a settlor could effect ten discretionary settlements which could, in aggregate, shelter a value of over £2 million without attracting any IHT. It has to be said, however, that the Revenue reaction to this kind of exercise is unknown and that it could prove somewhat provocative to them.

4.23 In summary, the advantages of a discretionary trust are:

- distributions of income or capital can be made according to the needs and circumstances of beneficiaries as they occur over the life of the trust;

- a wide range of beneficiaries can be included, say, the settlor's spouse;

- income can be accumulated for up to 21 years;

- the rates of income tax and CGT could be lower than those of the settlor or the potential beneficiaries;

- all assets transferred to such a trust are eligible for CGT hold-over relief.

4.24   The disadvantages are:

- the administration required;
- a discretionary trust is the most vulnerable of all types of trusts to changes in tax law;
- a transfer into the trust could attract lifetime IHT;
- there maybe periodic special IHT charges every ten years.

4.25   If death occurs within seven years of the chargeable lifetime transfer, additional tax may be payable, since tax is recomputed at the 40% rate, taking into account other chargeable transfers. Note that any potentially exempt transfers (PETs) made in the seven years before death become chargeable transfers. Any tax which becomes due on death on potentially exempt transfers or chargeable transfers, is reduced if the donor survives the transfer by more than three years. Thus it is reduced to 80% if death occurs in the fourth year, 60% in the fifth year and 20% in the sixth year.

4.26   The transfer of certain business property is exempt from IHT as long as these assets have been owned for at least two years prior to death. A most useful aspect of this, as far as financial advisers are concerned, is that alternative investment market (AIM) shares qualify as business property subject to one or two exceptions, principally dealing in land and buildings or holding investments.

Insurance and IHT

4.27   What can be done to cater for the possibility of death occurring within that seven-year period? There may well be serious IHT implications because PETs become chargeable transfers, and this can impact on other transfers.

4.28   Life assurance has a significant role to play here. If policies are written under trust, large IHT-free funds can be left on death and such funds can be used to pay any IHT liability which arises.

4.29   Term assurance is particularly useful in the case of PETs. The premiums are relatively cheap since a policy only pays out if the person whose life is insured actually dies within the seven-year period. Premiums can be reduced even further by using decreasing term assurance. Here the sum assured decreases each year from years four to seven to take account of the reducing potential IHT liability.

4.30 Term cover may also be considered where a donor makes an actual chargeable transfer, as death within the seven-year period following the transfer will result in death rates (subject to tapering relief) rather than lifetime rates being applicable. The position may be further worsened where the chargeable transfer is made after a potentially exempt transfer. The death of a donor, who has made both potentially exempt transfers and subsequent chargeable transfers in the seven years before his death, will necessitate the re-calculation of the inheritance tax payable on the chargeable transfers. The IHT on the chargeable transfers will originally have been calculated on the basis that the potentially exempt transfers were exempt. This has to be corrected since the potentially exempt transfers will come into account as prior chargeable transfers if made within the previous seven years.

4.31 The existence of chargeable transfers in the seven years prior to the donor's death may also affect the amount of tax payable on the donor's estate because the earlier transfers will be brought into account. Therefore, consideration should be given to taking out seven-year level term assurance to cover the increased amount of tax payable by the personal representatives, and putting the policy in trust for the donor's residuary beneficiaries under his will who can then use the proceeds to help fund the tax.

4.32 Since the premiums are relatively modest they can usually be funded by the person whose life is covered, since they will be deemed to be gifts out of normal expenditure.

4.33 Whole-life policies which provide for a capital sum to be paid only on the death of the insured, are often employed to fund the likely inheritance tax payable on death, in respect of an individual's estate, regardless of when the death occurs. When is advising a married couple, the basic question to be decided is which of the two lives should be insured – the first to die or the survivor.

4.34 The answer will depend on when the main (or only) inheritance tax charge will fall. Whole-life policies can be applicable in either situation. The appropriate policy when insuring the life of the survivor is a joint life and survivor policy.

4.35 Whole-life cover is the best way of establishing a fund which will grow over the years and will be available to fund the anticipated IHT charge on death, but the provision of such cover (particularly full cover) is usually expensive, except for young individuals. Also, whilst the level of cover is likely to be fixed by reference to the IHT payable, should the life assured die immediately after the policy is taken out, regard should be had to the likely increases in the assured's estate through income accumulation, capital growth and inflation and augmentation by gifts or legacies. A level of cover which originally seemed appropriate may, after a number of years, become inadequate (even with the addition of bonuses). The amount of cover should always be kept under review.

4.36 We have already hinted that the timing of gifts can be important. Generally speaking, it is better to make a PET before a chargeable transfer. This is because, if death occurs within seven years, the annual exempt amount is set first against the gift which was made first. If the PET is made after the chargeable transfer, this will often have the effect of bringing it fully into account for IHT purposes, while any IHT that was paid at the time of the chargeable transfer goes largely unrelieved. If the PET is made first, any IHT paid on the chargeable transfer tends to be taken fully into account.

Husband and wife planning

4.37 Many couples simply leave all of their assets to the other. This would appear to be a reasonable strategy since it avoids any IHT at the time of the first death. However, this usually results in more tax being paid on the second death than need be. This is because one of the nil rate bands is not utilised. A simple example illustrates the point. Suppose A and B both have an estate of £500,000, and each leaves everything to the other. Say that A dies first. B's estate now becomes £1 million. All other things being equal, when B dies, after taking their annual exempt amount into account, IHT will be payable on £750,000 – £300,000.

4.38 If A had left £250,000, say, to their children, there is still no IHT to pay on their death – the £250,000 going to B is an exempt transfer between husband and wife and the balance left to the children is within A's annual exempt allowance. B's estate is now worth £750,000 of which £500,000 will be taxable on their death, giving rise to an IHT charge of £200,000. This simple strategy saves £100,000 of IHT.

4.39 If the estate is not large enough or liquid enough to transfer £250,000 to children and grandchildren and still leave enough money for the surviving spouse, A can set up a discretionary trust, either whilst alive or via his will, and transfer £250,000 into it to utilise the nil rate band. B can be a beneficiary of this trust, and A can leave a letter of wishes to the trustees informing them that the main intention of setting up the trust is to ensure the financial comfort of the surviving spouse.

4.40   Trustees are not bound by such a letter since, by definition of the trust, they run it at their sole discretion. However, they will usually take account of the wishes of the person setting it up. In this way a surviving spouse can benefit without receiving the money as an outright gift. Since it is in trust it does not fall into B's estate on her death.

4.41   The family home is often a major asset. IHT planning concerning the family home can be fraught with legal difficulty and is considered later. However, there is one simple strategy that married couples should consider.

4.42   Firstly, they should organise matters so that the house is a joint holding between the two of them as tenants in common. This means that each of them has a separate, say, half, share which they can leave separately by will or dispose of during the lifetime.

4.43   This contrasts with the more usual type of ownership where joint owners are joint tenants. Under this method, the survivor automatically takes the entire interest absolutely on the death of the other. In the absence of any evidence to the contrary, where a property is in joint ownership, it will be deemed to be a joint tenancy.

4.44   In order to create a tenancy in common, both parties must say in writing that this is the way they want the property to be held. Each can leave their own half to the children. On the first death, the survivor can continue to occupy the whole of the property. As long as the will has been drafted very carefully, to avoid creating what is known as an interest in possession, the half that has been left to the children should not fall into the survivor's estate when they die. A very simple strategy is for the surviving parent to pay a fair rent for the half they do not own. This might be particularly appropriate in the case of children who are not using their personal tax allowances.

Pensions and IHT

4.45   We now consider benefits payable on death under an occupational pension scheme. Usually, any lump sum payable on death will not be subject to IHT since such benefit is normally payable at the discretion of the pension fund trustees and, therefore, falls outside the deceased's estate.

4.46   An individual can indicate whom they wish to receive the benefit, by giving a letter of wishes to the trustees. This will not be binding on them but they will usually honour it.

4.47 If a scheme provides for an adequate widow's pension, a lump sum death benefit could in this way be paid or applied for the benefit of a member's children. This could be a useful and IHT-free way for a member to provide for his dependants. Furthermore, by leaving to his wife the bulk of his free estate, the member could so arrange his affairs that very little (if any) IHT will be payable on his death, while at the same time he will have made adequate provision (within his means) for his dependants.

4.48 An extension to this approach might involve the use of a separate settlement to receive the death benefit. For example, the member could indicate that he wished the benefit to be paid to the trustees of a discretionary settlement (to be created, for example, by his will), the beneficiaries of that settlement including his wife and children. His wife could receive the income deriving from the lump sum, at the discretion of the trustees of the settlement, without the lump sum itself forming part of her estate on her death. The lump sum could then be used to meet some (if not all) of the eventual IHT liability on her death (depending, of course, on the terms of the trust) or it could be distributed to the next generation.

4.49 The disadvantage, however, of such a discretionary trust would be that the lump sum would be subject to the IHT regime applicable to such trusts. Generally speaking, IHT would be charged on the value of property comprised in the settlement on each ten-year anniversary of the commencement of the settlement. Additionally, there could be a charge to IHT on property leaving the settlement.

4.50 Inland Revenue rules mean it is possible that a ten-year charge could arise fairly soon after death and trustees of such separate discretionary trusts should be aware of this possibility. It is likely, however, that the tax saving on the death of the surviving spouse will far outweigh any such charge which might arise. At current rates, the maximum ten-year charge can only be 6% at most whilst the saving in tax on the death of the surviving spouse by using a separate discretionary trust, of which she is a beneficiary rather than paying the benefit to her, may well be 40% of the lump sum benefit.

Product opportunities

- Term Assurance

- Whole Life Assurance

Chapter 5

Advanced Mitigation of Income Tax

Property reversions

5.1 Those who do not want income from their investments should consider the purchase of a property subject to a home reversion. Home reversions are a form of equity release whereby an elderly person sells their property in return for a cash lump sum. They are granted a rent-free lifetime tenancy, and are required to repair, maintain and insure the property. On their death the property reverts to the purchaser to do with as they will.

5.2 How much an investor pays for a home reversion property obviously depends on the age of the occupant. Typically, if they are male and 70 years of age the purchase price will be 40% of market value, rising to 55% for someone aged 80. The discounts are slightly larger in the case of female occupants, since women have a longer life expectancy. In the case of a couple, the discount will be based on the younger of the two.

5.3 The yield on reversion properties cannot be calculated exactly, since it depends upon how long the tenants live. With a decent spread of such a property it is perfectly possible to achieve an effective return of about 10% per annum compound. The gain on the property, when it is realised, is subject to CGT. For taper relief purposes, the investment is dealt with as a personal rather than a business asset.

Funded unapproved retirement benefit scheme

5.4 Those clients running profitable family companies can reduce tax on rental income from property and any CGT via a funded unapproved retirement benefit scheme (FURBS).

5.5 What is a FURBS? Like most pension funds a FURBS is a trust with trustees who make investment decisions. Do not be put off by the word 'unapproved' – this simply means that it does not qualify for certain exemptions available to approved pension schemes.

Nevertheless, FURBS are recognised by the Inland Revenue and have some attractive advantages.

5.6   With a conventional approved scheme, there is a limit to the amount of benefit which can be taken, and the contributions that can be made. However, the funds grow tax-free. Employer contributions are not taxed on the employee and tax relief is available to the employee for personal contributions, subject to a limit of 15% of earnings.

5.7   The main advantages of a FURBS are:

- there are few restrictions on contributions into the scheme;
- the value within the fund can be paid out in full as a tax-free lump sum on retirement or death in service;
- the fund can be used to provide retirement benefits for dependants and others in excess of those available under an approved scheme;
- retirement may be any age after leaving service (even beyond age 75);
- minimal restrictions on investment of the contributions;
- the fund value is not usually liable to IHT;
- the employer normally gets tax relief on contributions;
- the fund is, in normal circumstances, secure if the employer faces financial problems.

5.8   It is generally best for contributions into a FURBS to be made by the company, not the employee. Personal contributions do not qualify for tax relief, may lead to higher tax liabilities on any income in the FURBS, and taint the fund's IHT position.

5.9   The company is liable to national insurance on its contributions, and they are also taxable on the employee at their marginal rate. Remember though, that the company will receive corporation tax relief. If the company is profitable and making between £300,000 and £1.5 million per year, it will obtain relief at the rate of 32.5%.

5.10   A FURBS can be used to fund the ownership of a buy-to-let or second or holiday home. There are no borrowing restrictions with a FURBS. Other possible arrangements such as SIPPS or SSAS do not permit investment in residential property.

5.11   FURBS pay tax at 22% on income, 20% on bank interest, 10% on dividends and 34% on capital gains, subject to taper relief, over the annual exemption limit for trusts. This is currently £3,850.

5.12 What are the advantages to a clients in holding buy-to-let property within a FURBS rather than personally? Firstly, the rental income will be taxed at a flat rate of 22%, whereas if a property were held personally, the income would probably be taxed at 40%. Secondly, the effective rate of capital gains tax on any gain, once a property has been held for 10 years, will be 20.4% in a FURBS and 24% outside it. Remember also that the beneficiary of a FURBS can take 100% of the fund as a tax-free lump sum on retirement or death in service.

5.13 A FURBS has other attractions. The trustees can invest into the company's shares or make a loan back to the company itself. A conventional pension scheme usually provides a lump sum of up to four times salary for death in service. A FURBS can be very useful to enhance these benefits.

5.14 A FURBS can also be a useful alternative to paying a large bonus, particularly where the employee will be saving it. The investment and tax benefits of the funds within a FURBS make it beneficial, although of course the employee will not be able to draw on them until retirement or death.

Higher risk strategies

5.15 Enterprise Investment Schemes (EISs) and Venture Capital Trusts (VCTs) are two ways of sheltering income from tax.

5.16 Those who subscribe for new ordinary shares in an unquoted trading company – including AIM companies – can claim income tax relief at 20% on that investment. Some trading activities are specifically excluded, including providing finance, legal and accountancy services, leasing, property development, farming and market gardening, forestry and timber production and hotels or nursing and residential care homes.

5.17 The individual making the investment must not be connected with the company – that is be an employee or director of it, or controlling more than 30% of its capital.

5.18 The maximum amount on which an individual can claim relief in any tax year is £150,000, this limit being available to both husband and wife. Relief is given in the tax year when the shares are purchased, but one-half of the amount subscribed before 6 October in any tax year can be carried back for relief in the previous tax year, up to a maximum carry-back of £25,000. Although the tax saving from the carry-back claim is calculated by reference to the tax position of the earlier year, it reduces the tax liability of the tax year in which the shares are subscribed for, so that any interest on overpaid tax will run only from 31 January after the end of that tax year. The claim for carry-back must be made at the same time as the claim for relief, and the carry-back cannot increase the relief for a tax year to more than £150,000. The minimum subscription by a individual to one company is £500.

5.19   The shares must be held for a minimum of three years (five years for shares issued before 6 April 2000) otherwise the relief is withdrawn completely if the disposal is not at arm's length and the tax saving is lost on the amount received for an arm's length bargain. Relief is also withdrawn if the individual receives value from the company within one year before or three years after the issue of the shares. Relief is not withdrawn when a shareholder dies.

5.20   With an EIS investment all the eggs are in one basket. A VCT spreads the risk. VCTs are quoted companies holding at least 70% of their investment in shares they have subscribed for in unquoted companies trading mainly in the UK. These companies are subject to the same trading exclusions as with an EIS.

5.21   When new ordinary shares are subscribed for, income tax relief at 20% may be claimed on up to £100,000 of the amount subscribed each tax year.

5.22   The relief will be withdrawn to the extent that any of the shares are disposed of (other than to the holder's spouse, or after the holder's death) within three years. Where shares are acquired from a spouse, the acquiring spouse is treated as if he or she had subscribed for the shares.

5.23   Dividends from ordinary shares in VCTs are exempt from tax to the extent that not more than £100,000 in total of shares in VCTs are acquired each year (whether acquired by subscription or by purchase from another shareholder). Dividend tax credits are, however, not repayable.

Product opportunities

* Property Reversions
* FURBS
* EISs
* VCTs

Chapter 6

Advanced Mitigation of CGT

EISs and VCTs

6.1 We have already seen that these can be used to shelter income from tax. They also have CGT advantages. A claim may be made for all or any part of a chargeable gain on the disposal of any asset to be deferred to the extent that it is matched by a subscription for EIS shares within one year before and three years after the disposal. Gains may be deferred whether or not income tax relief was available on the EIS shares (in particular enabling owner/directors to obtain deferral relief where they subscribe for shares, with the deferral not being limited to gains of £150,000). The relief is only available if the investor is resident and ordinarily resident in the UK.

6.2 Deferral relief is not available where there are guaranteed exit arrangements.

6.3 The deferred gain (as distinct from the gain on the EIS shares, which is dealt with above) becomes chargeable on the disposal of the shares, other than to a spouse. The deferred gain is not triggered if the investor (or spouse to whom the shares have been transferred) dies. Where the gain is triggered, it may be further deferred by another EIS investment if the conditions are satisfied.

6.4 Gains arising on the disposal of VCT shares that were acquired by subscription or purchase up to the £100,000 limit in any year, are exempt from CGT (and any losses are not allowable). There is no minimum period for which the shares must be held.

6.5 A claim may be made, by someone resident or ordinarily resident in the UK, for all or any part of gains on the disposal of any assets to be deferred to the extent that they are reinvested, within one year before or one year after the disposal, in VCT shares on which income tax relief is given and which (where relevant) are still held at the time of the disposal. The deferred gains (not the gains on the VCT shares themselves) become chargeable if the VCT shares are disposed of (other than to a spouse). The deferred gain is not triggered by the death of the investor (or spouse to whom the shares have been transferred). Where deferred gains are triggered, they may again be deferred, if further reinvested in new VCT shares or EIS shares if the conditions are satisfied.

Deathbed planning

6.6 Generally speaking, IHT deathbed planning, once it has become clear that a person only has a short time to live, is limited in scope, since there will be no mitigation of the IHT payable on any lifetime gifts unless the donor survives for three years. There is, however, one CGT opportunity for married couples.

6.7 If one of a couple has assets with a large potential CGT liability, and their spouse has a limited life expectancy, those assets could be transferred to them, with an arrangement for them to be bequeathed back to the donor by will. The recipient receives them at original base cost, but they are uplifted to market value on death. Therefore, when they are transferred back to the original donor, a new base cost has been established. No CGT will have been paid – as we have seen this is superseded at death by IHT. There is also, of course, no IHT liability, since transfers between spouses are exempt.

Non-qualifying TEPs

6.8 There also seems to be an opportunity to reduce CGT by the purchase and sale of non-qualifying TEPs. Non-qualifying policies will be those with terms of less than ten years, single premium bonds and some unit-linked whole-of-life policies. Again, some qualifying policies become non-qualifying due to a breach of the qualifying rules by the original policyholder.

6.9 Whereas the proceeds of a qualifying TEP are liable to CGT only, those from a non-qualifying policy are liable to both income tax and CGT. However, the Capital Gains Act 1992 stipulates that an individual cannot be charged both income tax and CGT on the same gain. This is the nub of using TEPs to reduce CGT liabilities which arise elsewhere.

6.10 A simple example will illustrate how it works. Suppose a client who is a higher rate taxpayer has purchased a non-qualifying TEP for £320,000 and subsequently sells it for £317,000. Assume that premiums of £120,000 have been paid. On the sale there will be liability to income tax on £197,000 – that is the difference between the sale proceeds and the premiums paid, regardless of who paid them. This income tax liability will be at 18% – the difference between basic and higher rate tax – because basic rate liability is deemed to be satisfied. The actual liability will therefore be £35,460.

6.11 On the CGT front a loss of £200,000 is created. This is made up of the actual capital loss of £3,000 – the difference between purchase and sale price plus the £197,000 which has already been charged to income tax. This loss of £200,000 is available to be set off against other capital gains and is therefore worth £80,000. The actual cash cost to generate the loss is £38,460 (income tax paid plus loss on sale of policy).

6.12 There is a more aggressive interpretation of the situation arising from a note in the Inland Revenue CGT manual, issued for the guidance of its inspectors. This states:

> 'Any part of the consideration for disposal of an asset which has either been charged to tax as income, or taken into account in computing income, should be excluded from the consideration for the disposal of the asset in computing the chargeable gain or allowable loss.'

If we take the same example and use this interpretation, the income tax liability is still £35,460, but the loss for CGT purposes is the full purchase price of £320,000. This is because the whole of the £317,000 proceeds has already been taken into account in computing income. This £320,000 loss is worth £128,000 to a higher rate taxpayer for the same cash cost of £38,460.

6.13 This second interpretation becomes particularly attractive if policies are chosen where the premiums paid are as close as possible to the sale proceeds. If we use the same example as above but assume that the premiums paid are £300,000, then the income liable to tax will be just £17,000. At the rate of 18% this gives a bill for £3,060, rather than £35,460.

6.14 The downside of choosing such policies is that if this aggressive interpretation is successfully challenged by the Inland Revenue, and it proves necessary to revert to the basic interpretation, only minimal losses for CGT purposes are generated. In the example above these losses will be just £20,000, comprising the £3,000 actual loss on disposal and the £17,000 charged to income tax.

6.15 The basic interpretation seems fairly watertight – it is equitable that a gain can only be charged to tax once. The Revenue could attack the scheme on the grounds that it is artificial, but anyone is entitled to make an investment decision and then change their minds, either because they need to realise the cash or have found what they consider to be a more attractive investment proposition.

6.16   Another potential snag is that if an investor regularly buys and sells significant numbers of policies the Revenue might seek to treat the whole exercise as 'an adventure in the nature of trade'. If that were to be the case, it would become pointless since the result would simply be the establishment of a small trading loss to offset against other income.

The use of share options

6.17   We have seen that in order to establish a higher base price for shares, it is no longer possible to 'bed and breakfast' them. There must be a minimum of 30 days between sale and repurchase, or the transaction is ignored for CGT purposes. When the stock market is buoyant there is a danger that there might be a significant increase in value before repurchase. If clients are concerned about this, they can take out a call option on the shares. A call option is just a device that gives its holder the right, but not the obligation, to buy something at a fixed price. So, if a client takes out an option to buy shares at, say, £1, this is the price they will pay if they choose to exercise the option, even if the shares double in value during the option period. If the price falls, the option can simply be allowed to lapse.

6.18   The London International Financial Futures and Options Exchange (LIFFE) lists options on interest rate futures, government bonds, commodities, individual equities and the FTSE 100 index. A contract normally represents an option on 1000 shares of the underlying security.

6.19   Each option contract has an expiry date and expiry dates are fixed at three-monthly intervals. There are three possible cycles starting in January, February or March. Equity options can run for up to nine months.

6.20   There are some 70-odd shares in which it is possible to take out traded options. Each will operate on one of the above cycles. Information is carried in some national newspapers and on the LIFFE website. A typical entry might read as follows:

Option		Calls			Puts		
		Oct	**Jan**	**Apr**	**Oct**	**Jan**	**Apr**
Abbey National	1050	35.5	106.5	136	13	70.5	108.5
(1071)	1100	11.5	82	112.5	39.5	95	134

6.21   This means that Abbey National shares have a market price of 1071p, and options are available for a share price of 1050p or 1100p. Let us look at the 1050p call options. An investor can buy an option to acquire Abbey National shares at a price of 1050p, regardless of any increase in their value. For a price per share (premium) of 35.5p, the shares can be purchased at the fixed price up to October. For a premium of 106.5p, they can be purchased at 1050p any time up to the following January, and for a premium of 136p at any time up to the following April.

Alternative investment market

6.22   Any investment in alternative investment market (AIM) shares has CGT attractions since such shares are classed as business assets. For a higher rate taxpayer, therefore, the effective rate of CGT on any gain is just 10% once the shares have been held for at least two years.

6.23   AIM shares are obviously not a low risk investment, and any client going down this route would be advised to select a portfolio of such shares so that the risk is spread. The following general guidelines may aid selection.

6.24   An extended track record is useful. Most AIM companies are well-established businesses with historical track records on which they can be analysed. If clients are averse to the potential risks of start-up or seed companies, they should probably only consider investing in those with trading records of more than three years.

6.25   Many AIM stocks, particularly those in the technology sector, suffer in terms of their perceived market valuation due to the fact that it is often difficult to compare them with any similar quoted business.

6.26   As far as valuation and forecasts are concerned, concentrate on the first 12 months and pay little attention to three- or five-year forecasts. Forecasts from the company's house broker will obviously carry more weight than outside forecasts.

6.27 Directors and institutional share dealings are often good buy/sell indicators.

6.28 The availability of shares – liquidity may not be good. Some AIM companies make as little as 10% of their share capital available to the public. This means that the share price will be very sensitive. Unless your clients enjoy roller coaster rides, they should stay clear of those stocks with less than 25% of their share capital in public hands.

6.29 Some fund managers and stockbrokers who specialise in smaller companies offer an AIM portfolio selection service. This is very useful for those who do not relish the prospect of selecting AIM stocks themselves.

6.30 The minimum subscription amount is typically £50,000 and each client has a bespoke portfolio which might well contain 30 holdings.

Employee share schemes

6.31 There are no less than six different types of share schemes currently available for employees.

6.32 On the CGT front, shares acquired will usually count as business assets. They will, therefore, qualify for the maximum of 75% taper relief, after two years. The effective CGT rate for a higher rate taxpayer is, therefore, 10%.

Unapproved share option schemes

6.33 An employee has an option to buy shares in the future at a price which is normally fixed when the option is granted. There are no limits on the value of options which can be issued and no restrictions on the price at which the shares can be offered.

6.34 There is no income tax or national insurance (NI) liability when the options are granted as long as they are required to be exercised within ten years of being granted. An income tax charge arises when the option is exercised, based on the difference between market value at the date of exercise, and the exercise price.

6.35 When the shares are sold, any further gain will be subject to CGT, with the base cost being the market value of the shares when the option was exercised.

Approved share option schemes

6.36   The value of options which can be held by one employee is limited to £30,000, and the exercise price must be the approximate market value of the shares when the option was actually granted. Options can only be exercised tax-free once every three years, and cannot be exercised more than ten years after they were granted.

6.37   There is no tax charge on either grant or exercise. When the shares are eventually sold, any gain is subject to CGT. The base cost will be the exercise price, not the market value at the date of exercise.

SAYE share option schemes

6.38   Such schemes link an approved option scheme to an SAYE savings contract. Options may be granted at a discount of up to 20% of market value at the time of grant. Employees can save between £5 and £250 per month for either three, five or seven years. At the end of this period, the proceeds can be used to fund the acquisition of shares, or the employee can take the proceeds in cash.

6.39   The tax situation is exactly the same as with other approved schemes, as outlined above. The interest earned on the savings contract, and any terminal bonus received, are exempt from income tax, whether or not the proceeds are used to buy shares.

Approved profit-sharing schemes

6.40   These must be operated using a dedicated trust. The employer makes payments to the trust to buy shares which are allocated free to employees. The maximum value of shares that can be given to an employee each year is £3,000 worth, or 10% of salary – excluding benefits and after deducting pension contributions – whichever is the greater. There is an overall maximum of £8,000 worth.

6.41   On the tax front, shares cannot be sold for the first two years. If they are sold in the third year, they are assessed to income tax and NI on their market value when allocated, or sale proceeds if less. Disposals after three years do not give rise to an income tax charge. Whenever the shares are disposed of, a CGT charge will arise based on the difference between the selling price and the value when the shares were given to the employee.

Enterprise incentive management schemes

6.42 These allow tax favoured share options to be granted to employees in companies with gross assets of no more than £15 million. Up to £3 million worth of options can be granted in total, but no employee can have more than £100,000 worth.

6.43 No tax or NI is payable on the grant of the option as long as it can be and is exercised within ten years. Similarly, there is no charge when the option is exercised as long as the option price is at least equal to the market value of the shares when it was granted.

6.44 CGT is chargeable on the profit element on the sale of shares. However, taper relief will run from the date an option is granted, not the date the shares are acquired.

Share incentive plans (originally known as all-employee share ownership plans)

6.45 Employers can give up to £3,000 of shares free to an employee each year. In addition, employees can buy partnership shares up to £1,500 per year. When employees exercise this option, the employer can give free matching shares up to a maximum of two for each partnership share. Dividends can be re-invested, subject to a maximum of £1,500 each tax year.

6.46 There are no tax and NI contributions when the shares are acquired. If the shares are held for five years (dividend shares three years), they can be withdrawn free of income tax and NI. Shares retained for at least five years are only subject to CGT on sale. The gains are calculated according to the rise in value of the shares from the date they were withdrawn from the plan to the date of sale.

6.47 For some schemes it is possible to escape a CGT charge completely by transferring shares directly into a self-select ISA. This applies to shares acquired under a SAYE scheme, an approved profit sharing scheme and a share incentive plan. Transfer must be effected within 90 days of the shares passing to the individual. Any capital gain which arises on transfer into the ISA is tax-free. Subject to the allowance being unused, £7,000 worth can be transferred in each tax year.

6.48 The merits of this need to be weighed up carefully, particularly if the shares have been held long enough to qualify for full taper relief.

It may be better to utilise the ISA allowance for other investments and suffer tax at 10%. The first £7,700 worth of total capital gains each year is exempt from CGT anyway. Remember too, that in an all-employee share ownership plan, gains are shielded from CGT as long as they remain in the plan.

6.49 In terms of portfolio balance, it may not be a good idea for clients to have a large number of shares in their employing company. Consideration should be given to realising shares up to the CGT exempt limit and investing more widely. Shares can be transferred to a spouse before sale to enable them to utilise their CGT exempt limit too. It is probably not tax-efficient to gift such shares to a spouse if they have used their exempt allowance. The benefit of business taper relief will be lost.

6.50 One final point – even if clients have acquired shares in their employing company other than through a scheme, any capital gain on sale will be subject to business taper relief.

Product opportunities

- EIS
- VCT
- Non-qualifying TEPs
- Share Options
- AIM Shares
- Self-Select ISAs

Chapter 7

Advanced Mitigation of IHT

Interest in possession settlements

7.1   For those who wish to retain control of assets given away or do not wish the intended beneficiary to acquire full control following the gift, at least until a later date, an interest in possession trust may provide a solution. This is an alternative to a discretionary trust, where the settlor is happy for the beneficiary to have a right to the income from the trust.

7.2   Interest in possession is a concept of general trust law and there is no statutory definition. Case law, however, has decided that an interest in possession exists where one or more of the beneficiaries has a right to the trust income as it arises or to the use or enjoyment of the trust property. Examples will include the right to income for life, or, say, until remarriage, or the right to occupy a freehold property rent-free during a lifetime.

7.3   Any absolute lifetime gift to an interest in possession trust, where the settlor does not retain an interest, is a PET, so no IHT is payable as long as the donor survives for seven years. Potential exemption is also available where an interest in possession in settled property comes to an end during the life of the individual entitled to it, as long as someone else becomes entitled to the property absolutely or to an interest in possession in it.

7.4   On the income tax front, the trustees are charged to tax on dividend income at 10%, on savings income at the lower rate of 20% and on other income at the basic rate (currently 22%). Trustees are not liable to higher rate tax. Income is calculated in the same way as for an individual. There are, however, no deductions for personal allowances. There is no relief for expenses of managing the trust, which are therefore paid out of the after-tax income. They are treated as paid out of savings income in priority to non-savings income and out of dividend income before other savings income.

7.5   The beneficiaries entitled to the income are personally liable to income tax on it, whether they draw the income or leave it in the trust fund (assuming the settlor has not retained an interest). They are entitled to a credit for the tax paid by the trustees, but in relation to dividends the credit is non-repayable.

7.6   If the settlor transfers chargeable assets to the trust, they are liable to CGT on transfer unless they are qualifying business assets. Gains arising within the trust are taxed at 34%, subject to an annual exemption (currently £3,850).

7.7   When a beneficiary becomes absolutely entitled to trust property following the death of the person entitled to the income, the trustees are regarded as disposing of the property to the beneficiary at its then market value, but no CGT liability arises. Any increase in value up to that time escapes CGT (and any losses are not allowable). A tax-free uplift for capital gains tax also occurs on property that remains in the trust after the death of the person entitled to the income.

7.8   When a life interest terminates other than on death, for example because a widow remarries, but the property remains in trust, there is neither a chargeable gain nor a change in the base value of the property for future capital gains tax disposals by the trustees.

7.9   When, however, a beneficiary becomes absolutely entitled to trust property other than on the death of the person entitled to the income, this is regarded as a disposal at market value at that date, and capital gains tax is payable on the increase in value, subject to any available indexation allowance and taper relief.

7.10   An interesting planning opportunity arises in the case of shares in a family company. This hinges on the fact that the IHT rules allow beneficial ownership and interest in possession entitlement to be valued separately. For example, if an individual owns, say, 40% of the ordinary shares in the family company outright and 40% by way of a life interest, the two 40% holdings will be valued on their death as two minority shareholdings, and not as part of an 80% controlling interest.

IHT and the family home

7.11   Often the family home is the most valuable asset and substantial IHT is payable, even when the deceased has only limited assets. Passing on to the children the family home, or a share of it, as a lifetime IHT planning strategy is appealing because it does not involve financial 'loss'. It is not possible simply to give the home away and continue to live in it due to the reservation with benefit provisions – assets given away are still treated as belonging to the donor if they continue to enjoy any benefit from them. There are schemes to get round this. Beware, however, that the Inland Revenue is likely to challenge these.

7.12 The home can be sold to another member of the family but subject to a lease/tenancy retained by the vendor for a number of years while the new owner pays a very small rent. The property should be sold at market value, but, since it is subject to lease, its market value will be considerably less than otherwise. The purchaser should pay from their own resources or independent financing.

7.13 The owner retains a share of the home and gives the rest to his/her children or to trustees of the children's settlement. Each joint owner must occupy the home and pay due share of its running. If the children later move away, the original owner will have to pay a full rent or be seen as starting reservation of benefit. This problem can be avoided if the child moving out grants the parent(s) a life interest in their share.

7.14 It may be possible to base an arrangement on a gift of cash. For example, a father could give his son £80,000 with which he buys a home where father and son then both live. The reservation of benefit rules do not apply to such an outright cash gift or the proceeds. The gift must be an absolute, outright gift, not into settlement.

7.15 It would be unrealistic, however, if the cash were used to buy the estate owner's existing home. The Inland Revenue would attack that either as an associated operation or on the grounds of the arrangements being too artificial.

7.16 A judicious interval should be left between the time of the cash gift and the start of occupation of the new home, say six months, and preferably straddling a 5 April tax year end.

7.17 A much simpler strategy is to reduce the value of the home by mortgage. If a couple are reluctant to move, but still wish to give away during their lifetime some of the accumulated value of their home, they may be able to do so by borrowing against its value and giving away the proceeds. This is only feasible if there are sufficient funds available from other sources to service the borrowing. On death the outstanding mortgage debt will be deductible for IHT purposes, albeit that the debt itself will still have to be met by the estate.

7.18 Where the donors are prepared to give away a property, for example, a second home, without ever wishing to occupy it again, then the IHT position is, by comparison, straightforward – but a CGT charge will arise.

7.19 As in all lifetime planning, but especially in the case of the family home, the primary concern will be for the financial and residential security of the owner or owners – tax saving should always take second place. For this reason, lifetime estate planning for the family home is often very limited in scope and the individuals concerned may be better advised to use other assets.

Business property relief

7.20 For transfers during lifetime or on death of a business, or an interest in a business, including a partnership share, or transfers out of unquoted shareholdings, including AIM shares, there is 100% relief from IHT as long as the property transferred has been owned by the donor for the previous two years.

Posthumous will variation

7.21 If someone dies either intestate or not having disposed of their assets in the most IHT-efficient manner, can anything be done?

7.22 Those entitled to a deceased's estate, either as a result of a will or an intestacy, can all agree to vary the way in which it is distributed. Any beneficiary can also turn down an entitlement or redirect it elsewhere. This must be done within two years of the testator's death. In the case of beneficiaries under 18, court consent is necessary for a variation. This can take some time so should be put in hand well before the end of the two-year period. It is also advisable to have any variation effected by a solicitor.

7.23 Any assets which are willed to a spouse are exempt from IHT. However, as we have seen, this can often mean that one of them does not make use of their nil rate band. Consider the following example. Emily dies, leaving all her assets to her husband Harry. Emily's assets are £350,000 and Harry's are £150,000. No IHT is payable when Emily dies but there is a potential liability when Harry dies. His assets are now £500,000 and tax will be payable on the excess over £250,000 – that is £250,000 at 40% = £100,000. The benefit of Emily's nil rate band has been totally lost.

7.24 The way to remedy this situation where there are children, is for Harry to arrange a variation of Emily's will to pass £250,000 directly to the children with the balance of £100,000 still going to him. There is still no IHT payable on Emily's death. Harry's estate has reduced to £250,000 and there is no IHT liability on this either enabling £100,000 to be saved.

7.25 There is a problem with the above if Harry needs the income of the estate to live on. In this case, if Emily has made no gifts within seven years of her death, he can vary her will to put the £250,000 in a discretionary trust for the benefit of himself and the children. He can then benefit from the income, but if he dies within ten years of Emily, the trust can be wound up and the capital distributed to the children. In most cases no IHT will be payable, regardless of the value of the trust fund. There are further IHT implications if the trust exists for ten years. If Harry is still alive then, a decision needs to be taken as to whether it should be continued or not.

7.26 Another opportunity to reduce IHT liability arises when a deceased's estate increases in value in the two years after death. A simple example of this is where a man dies worth £250,000, leaving it all to his wife. Say the estate doubles in value over the next 18 months. The widow can vary the will so that her legacy is £250,000 with the residue passing to her children. This means that £250,000 passes to the children tax-free and the IHT situation remains the same because the estate's value at the date of death was only £250,000. The widow's estate, however, has been reduced by £250,000 and the potential IHT liability on her death by £100,000.

7.27 Beneficiaries may wish to vary a will to give a fairer distribution of the deceased's assets. Children, for example, may wish to transfer part of their entitlement to a surviving parent who has inadequate means. Wealthy beneficiaries may wish to pass any legacy onto their own children – generation skipping. An estate may receive a claim under the *Inheritance Act* which allows anyone who was maintained by the deceased to apply for adequate provision. The beneficiaries may feel that a variation is preferable to protracted haggling and a court application by the claimant. If there is a typing error or some descriptive mistake in the will it is usually cheaper to re-write the defective part by variation than to apply to the court.

Chapter 8

Offshore Strategies

Introduction

8.1 This chapter concerns itself with offshore strategies. The main reason for investing offshore is the potential saving in income tax, CGT or IHT. Historically, the term offshore has been synonymous with money laundering, tax evasion and sleaze. However, UK investors who invest money offshore do so perfectly legally and are not evading tax. Investing offshore can be a very efficient tax option, particularly for those who are higher rate taxpayers. Offshore investment is simply one with a product provider who is outside the jurisdiction of the UK. This offers investors the opportunity to choose when they pay tax on their investments.

Offshore bonds

8.2 All offshore centres offer the same tax advantages. They differ only in the levels of investment protection that they provide and the products that they offer. The most popular product is the pooled funds insurance-based offshore bond. A pooled fund is essentially one that invests in unit trusts and investment trusts. The main attraction of such bonds is that they grow free of income tax and CGT in a process known as 'gross roll-up'. There is usually only a small amount of withholding tax to be paid and the income and capital growth are not taxed until an encashment is made.

8.3 For those requiring a regular income, tax-deferred withdrawals can be made of up to 5% per annum of the original investment up to a maximum of 100% of the original sum. As with UK bonds, this 5% element can be cumulative. Thus an investor can withdraw nothing for five years and then take 30% in year six without incurring any immediate tax liability. Another advantage of bonds is that they only ever give rise to an income tax liability on the investor, never a CGT liability. This means that a bond can be viewed as a 'wrapper' for a range of investment funds, and these funds may be switched without realising a tax liability at that time. This would not be the case with investments that are liable to CGT.

8.4 Non-pooled fund insurance bonds are not suitable for UK resident investors, due to their penal and complex taxation.

8.5 Any annual income in excess of 5% taken on a bond will be liable to income tax at the taxpayer's marginal rate for that year. When the bond is cashed in, investors are liable to income tax on the total gain at their relevant rate, less any tax already paid on withdrawals over 5% per annum. This gives an investor the ability to cash in and pay tax, say, after retirement when they are likely to be in a lower tax band.

8.6 Bonds are often segmented into a number of different policies so that they can be encashed piecemeal to avoid moving a basic rate taxpayer into the higher tax bracket in the year of encashment. If encashment of a policy would move a basic rate taxpayer into the higher bracket, top slicing relief is available which spreads the gain over the life of the bond. This usually means that the whole of the gain is taxed at the basic rate.

8.7 What about other situations where an offshore investment product may be suitable?

Non-taxpayers

8.8 Non-taxpayers would not suffer any tax liability on encashment on any gain within their personal allowance. Coupled with the 5% withdrawal facility this could represent a valuable level of 'tax deferred' income. This could be useful, for example, for university expenses or for maximising the opportunities under separate assessment by arranging for the policy to be effected by a non-earning spouse.

8.9 The 2002–03 personal allowance is £4,615, which, combined with the 5% allowance, means that a single premium investment of up to £92,300 can provide an income of £9,230 i.e. 10% per annum without any immediate liability to tax.

CGT planning for wealthy individuals

8.10 Since life policies do not normally come within the remit of the CGT legislation, for those investors who are already utilising their annual CGT exemption, an offshore bond can present an excellent opportunity to maximise the investment potential without restricting holdings to the long investment periods required to benefit fully from taper relief.

IHT planning

8.11 This can range from simple utilisation of the nil rate band through protection and gifting to sophisticated plans which allow the investor to enjoy a degree of access to their capital without falling foul of the gift with reservation provisions.

Trustee investments

8.12 Like individuals, trustees need to build up substantial capital sums to meet future expenditure in the form of providing benefits to future beneficiaries. The problem, however, is that, unlike individuals, they do not have access to UK based tax efficient investment such as ISAs. Furthermore, they currently have no personal allowance for income tax and enjoy only a CGT allowance equal to half (or less) that available to individuals. Income tax is payable by trustees at basic rate, or 34%, dependent on type of trust and capital gains are always taxed at 34%.

8.13 Depending on the needs of the trust, an offshore life policy can represent an excellent investment vehicle. Life policies are non-income producing assets, therefore in the hands of UK resident trustees they do not generate an ongoing income tax or CGT charge. A tax charge only arises when benefits are taken and will usually fall on the settlor of the trust. This can be useful when the settlor is a non-taxpayer. When the settlor is deceased the tax charge will fall on the trustees. If they are outside the UK, the tax charge will fall on UK beneficiaries, but only when they receive benefits.

8.14 Offshore bonds can also be useful for critical illness cover. Disability is not a chargeable event under the life policy tax rules. Accordingly, there is no gain calculation and no income tax charge when a policy providing critical illness cover becomes payable due to a claim. Thus cover might be provided at more beneficial rates than onshore. Similarly, long-term care cover might be funded offshore at lower premium rates than onshore.

8.15 However, with these products, as indeed with all offshore products, an investor must carefully weigh up the pros and cons of offshore against onshore. Premiums are certainly one important factor, but so too are benefits. It is also important to consider the financial strength and management of the actual company selected for an investment.

8.16 Offshore products generally carry higher charges than onshore bonds or unit trusts. An offshore bond typically charges an initial 8% compared to 5% onshore. The annual management fee might be 1.25% against the onshore product's 0.75%. However, the effect of such charges should be mitigated in the medium to long term as the benefits of gross roll-up become evident. The charging structures from company to company can be very difficult to compare. Investors should check the reduction in yield figures in providers' documentation in order to assess the true impact of their charges.

8.17 As far as the income tax return is concerned, offshore bonds do not need to be included until they are encashed, or income in excess of 5% is taken in any tax year. This contrasts with offshore investment and deposit accounts where interest and dividends received must be recorded each year and UK tax paid.

Offshore deposit accounts

8.18 On the bank and building society deposit front, there is little point in UK taxpayers holding an offshore account. There are only marginal benefits over onshore. There might be a short-term advantage since interest is paid gross. There is thus a compounding effect during the delay between interest being credited and the tax bill having to be paid. If interest is credited, say, in mid-April one year the tax on it will not be due until the following April. This is only likely to be significant where large sums of cash are involved. Furthermore, interest rates on sterling accounts are quite likely to be more favourable in the UK than offshore.

Offshore unit trusts

8.19 For investment funds, there is little benefit for a UK taxpayer investing in an offshore unit trust fund. Such funds fall into two types, distributor and non-distributor, depending upon whether or not they pay out dividends. Most distributor funds are taxed in the same way as their UK counterparts, hence there is no tax advantage and no point in suffering the higher management charges. Non-distributor funds are taxed in the same way as offshore bonds – all income and capital gain taxed as income on encashment. However, unlike an offshore bond, it is not possible to make a withdrawal from a non-distributor fund without incurring an immediate tax liability.

Offshore bespoke trust

8.20   Such a trust is an arrangement whereby a capital fund is created and maintained as a quite independent legal entity from the person creating the fund. The normal objective of an offshore trust is to place capital outside the present country of residence of the principals. This fund can be held free of exchange control, and other political or economic restrictions which might be imposed now, or in the future, in the country of residence of the individual, or intended recipients of the income or capital from the fund.

8.21   The parties to a trust are the settlor, the beneficiaries, the trustees and the protector. A trust deed will set out the duties and powers of the various parties. The beneficiaries may include the settlor, the spouse, children, grandchildren, any future children not yet born, or any other parties the settlor may propose. The trust deed can be updated at any time in the future and it is quite possible that the initial deed will not list any of the eventual beneficiaries.

8.22   The trustees actually manage the affairs of the trust and it is quite usual to appoint professionals or a corporate entity managed by a professional firm authorised to act as a trustee. The settlor may like an independent third party to monitor the trustees, in which case a protector may be appointed. This will usually be a trusted friend or professional advisor of the settlor. The protector can appoint and remove trustees and nominate additional beneficiaries.

8.23   The potential problem with a sole protector is that the authorities within his country could influence actions with regard to the appointment of trustees. This could result in the tax residence of the trust being changed. This can be overcome by appointing a Council of Four, consisting of four individuals resident in four different countries and acting by a majority. This gives continuity beyond the life of any one protector, and security. No one country can block the action of the Council and no two countries can force action. This protection against political change can be useful if, say, the country of residence of the trustees suddenly imposes exchange control restrictions, requiring a change of management of the trust to an alternative jurisdiction.

8.24   The most popular trust in offshore tax planning is a discretionary trust. Accumulation and maintenance trusts are almost always established for the benefit of the settlor's children. The deed will specify that the trust funds are to be used for the education and maintenance of children up to a certain age, at which point they are entitled to their share of the trust capital. The same result can often be achieved via a discretionary trust and, depending upon the tax residence position of the settlor and beneficiaries, this can give tax benefits.

8.25 Asset protection trusts have become popular as a result of the rapid increase of litigation against professional firms and the medical profession. As a result, many individuals have elected to create offshore trusts in which to place some of their assets, in the hope that they will be safe from any future claims. Tax saving opportunities are not normally a factor with these trusts.

8.26 An innovation in the trust world is the advent of purpose trusts. These are established for a specific purpose and no beneficiaries are identified. Their main use has been for charitable purposes and one-off commercial ventures.

8.27 Another option is a hybrid company. This looks like a company, but has many of the same features as a trust. A typical company will allow the shareholders to have voting and administrative powers, while the beneficial owners could be non-shareholding members in whom all the rights to income and capital are vested. A major benefit is that a company may be more readily accepted as an investing entity in some countries than a trust would be.

Specific benefits of using an offshore trust

Preservation of wealth and selected distribution of assets

8.28 Trusts will typically be used by individuals with substantial assets, who want to ensure that this wealth is distributed to their families in a manner of their choosing. With a discretionary trust the options available are numerous. The settlor may issue a letter of wishes, and update this as his own or family circumstances change. It is this flexibility which is one of the great attractions of a discretionary trust.

Favourable tax treatment

8.29 The major tax benefit in using a trust is that the assets held by a trust belong to the trustees and not to the settlor. By taking the assets out of the settlor's estate, they would normally cease to be taxable on the settlor. This can often be very useful for IHT purposes and for deferring capital gains. The tax benefits will depend on where the settlor and beneficiaries reside. For instance, any capital gains made by a trust established in Guernsey or the Isle of Man, and any income received by such a trust, would not be taxed by the authorities in its jurisdiction.

Forced heirship laws

8.30   Some countries have laws which determine how an individual's estate should be distributed on death. Such laws are known as forced heirship laws. Where some of the assets of an individual are held in such a country, it may be possible to use a trust to distribute those assets in a manner which would not be possible under the forced heirship laws.

Creditor protection

8.31   If an individual transfers part of their assets to an offshore trust, these assets cease to be part of the estate and, as such, any future claims by creditors will not normally be enforceable against the trustees. It is important to note that if the settlor creates the trust with the express intention of avoiding creditors, it is most likely that it will be set aside.

Anonymity

8.32   Isle of Man and Guernsey trusts, like most other trusts, are not required to file any information with the authorities, either on creation or on an annual basis. It is also possible to create the trust through a declaration of trust without identifying the settlor in the document itself.

Compensation schemes

8.33   The most popular offshore jurisdictions are Dublin, Guernsey, Isle of Man, Jersey and Luxembourg. The tax advantages and types of products are the same in each, but compensations schemes vary, as the following table indicates.

Jurisdiction	Depositor compensation scheme	Investor compensation scheme	Insurance compensation scheme
Dublin	Refunds lesser of 90% of total deposits or €20,000 per investor	Refunds lesser of 90% of total investment or €20,000 per investor.	No
Guernsey	No	90% of first £50,000, 30% of balance up to £100,000 per investor.	No

Jurisdiction	Depositor compensation scheme	Investor compensation scheme	Insurance compensation scheme
Isle of Man	75% of total deposits to a maximum refund of £15,000 per investor	100% of the first £30,000, 90% of next £20,000	Refunds 90% of insurer's liabilities to life insurance policyholders
Jersey	No	As in Isle of Man	No
Luxembourg	Refunds up to €20,000 per investor	Refunds up to €20,000 per investor	No

Offshore and the FSA

8.34   Advisers are only allowed to recommend FSA recognised funds, unless they know a client well and consider them to be an expert and experienced investor. The majority of these recognised funds are from other EU countries or other designated territories such as Jersey, Guernsey and the Isle of Man which have equivalent regulation to the UK.

Product opportunities

* Offshore Bonds
* Critical Illness Cover
* Offshore Deposit Accounts

Chapter 9

Investing for Children

Filling the piggy bank

9.1   Children have the same tax allowances as adults. These include a personal allowance and CGT exemption. Thus in the current year a child can earn £4,615 before becoming liable to income tax and can realise a tax-free capital gain of £7,700.

9.2   As a general rule, if a child is under 18 and unmarried, any income that arises on investments, directly or indirectly, made by a parent, is treated as the income of the parent. However, there are certain exceptions:

- Each parent can give each child a capital sum (say a bank or building society deposit) from which the child receives no more than £100 gross income per annum. (But if the income exceeded the limit, the whole amount and not just the excess over £100 would be taxed on the parent.)

- The national savings children's bonus bonds for under 16-year-olds can be given in addition.

- A parent may pay premiums (maximum £270 per annum) on a qualifying friendly society policy for a child under 18.

- From 6 April 2001 a parent may pay personal pension contributions of up to £3,600 a year on behalf of a child under 18, such contributions being paid net of basic rate tax, which is retained whether or not the child is a taxpayer. The pension fund is, of course, not available to the child until he/she reaches pension age.

- A parent may establish an accumulation and maintenance settlement for his children, the income from which is not treated as his in certain circumstances.

9.3   Interestingly, if a parent gifts an asset which produces capital growth, any capital gain is taxed as the child's. Therefore, there is an opportunity to invest on a child's behalf in a unit or investment trust which distributes little or no income and concentrates on capital growth.

9.4 If investments are made in the child's name absolutely, then the child has control and can realise the assets whenever they wish, and do with the money as they want. Secondly, there can be practical difficulties if a child holds certain securities, e.g. shares, in their own name. One reason for this is that a contract cannot be enforced against a minor. So problems might arise where, for example, shares are to be paid for in stages.

9.5 The way round this problem is to set up a trust. The two most common ones are a bare trust and an accumulation and maintenance trust. As mentioned above, the latter also gets round the problem of parents gifting income-producing assets to their children.

Bare trusts

9.6 The beneficiary has an absolute right to the assets and income, but the trustees are the legal owners and hold the property as a nominee. A bare trust can be a bank or building society account or shareholding in a parent's name with the child's interest noted. This can be achieved by appending the child's initials after the parent's name. Note that when the child reaches 18 it can insist on having the property transferred into its own ownership absolutely.

9.7 Where capital gains are made, a bare trust is entitled to the full annual exemption, rather than half of that amount as applies to other trusts. Furthermore, the transfer to a bare trust is a potentially exempt transfer for IHT, becoming completely exempt if the donor survives the seven-year period.

Accumulation and maintenance trusts

9.8 These are a special sort of discretionary trust.

9.9 The rule that a parent remains chargeable to income tax on income from funds settled on their own unmarried children under the age of 18, does not apply where the capital and income are held in accumulation and maintenance trusts for the benefit of children. The only exception to this is the extent to which any income is paid to or for the benefit of the child, say for education or maintenance.

9.10 Payments of capital to or for the benefit of the child are also treated as income to the extent that the trust fund has any undistributed income. Any such income or capital payments are treated as the parent's income and taxed on them – unless, together with any other income from the parent, they do not exceed £100 in any tax year.

9.11   Income received by the trustees before a beneficiary is entitled to it is chargeable at the rate applicable to trusts – 34% or 25% on gross UK dividend income. If the income is distributed to the beneficiaries, they may be able to recover all or part of that tax depending on their personal tax circumstances. As noted above, of course, if the beneficiaries are infant unmarried children of the settlor, income distributed will be assessed on the settlor until the children reach 18.

9.12   All trusts are subject to anti-avoidance legislation. In particular, the settlor should reserve no right to benefit personally from the fund and any dealings between the settlor and the trustees must be treated with extreme caution.

9.13   On the IHT front any transfer into the trust will be treated as potentially exempt and will therefore escape tax totally as long as the settlor survives for seven years.

9.14   On the CGT front a gift of chargeable assets into trust may give rise to a chargeable gain by the settlor. The exception to this is where the assets transferred are qualifying business assets, in which case an election can be made for hold-over relief. Disposal of assets by trustees are chargeable to CGT subject to an annual exemption for trusts of half the personal exemption. Any gains are charged to tax at the special rate applicable to trusts, i.e. 34%.

9.15   One advantage of an accumulation and maintenance trust over a bare trust is that provision can be made for beneficiaries as yet unborn. Under a bare trust, the amount held for each child must be fixed at the date it is set up, and cannot be varied. With an accumulation and maintenance trust, trustees can use their discretion to vary the size of each child's share and to defer the time when the child can receive capital.

9.16   To comply with IHT regulations there must be at least one beneficiary living when the trust is set up. However, a settlor with no children or grandchildren can 'borrow' a beneficiary, say a cousin, whom the trustees can be given power to exclude from benefit once 'genuine' beneficiaries are born.

Friendly societies

9.17 Friendly society savings plans have been a traditional way for parents and grandparents alike to put something by for their little ones.

9.18 The main reason for their popularity is their tax-free status. Savers can put away up to £25 a month or £270 a year tax-free under current tax legislation. When you consider that saving for children could keep going for as long as 21 years, it is possible to turn modest savings into meaningful rewards.

9.19 The best bit about this tax break is that parents, or other adults saving for a child, don't have to sacrifice their own friendly society tax allowance. With this type of savings plan a child can have one in their own right, even though someone else is saving on their behalf.

Children's Bonus Bonds

9.20 These are available from National Savings and Investments and parents simply invest a lump sum on behalf of a child. Children's Bonus Bonds are available in Issues and each has its own rate of return and a separate investment limit. From £25 to £1,000 can be invested each time there is a new Issue of Children's Bonus Bonds, in units of £25.

9.21 For five years the Bond will earn interest at a fixed rate. Then, on the fifth anniversary, a bonus is added which is fixed and guaranteed at the outset. At that point the person who controls the Bond can decide whether to cash it in, or leave it invested.

9.22 Children's Bonus Bonds are owned by the child. But until they reach 16 the Bond is controlled by their parent or guardian regardless of who bought it. This means only the parent or guardian can cash in the Bond, but the money still belongs to the child.

9.23 Normally, as we have seen, if a parent gives their child money to invest, the parent is liable to tax on the interest if it comes to over £100 in any tax year, even if the child is not a taxpayer. But with Children's Bonus Bonds the interest and bonuses are all completely tax-free. Even if the child starts work and becomes a taxpayer before cashing in their Bonds, there will still be no tax to pay on the interest.

Stakeholder pension

9.24 In a survey conducted in late 2001, 21% of parents said they would be likely to take out a stakeholder pension for their children.

9.25 The research, asked parents whether they were already saving regularly for their children's future. Their response showed that over half (57%) are saving at least £20 per month (per child).

9.26 When you factor in the tax benefits of a stakeholder (£100 gross contribution would cost parents/grandparents only £78), its flexibility and low cost is a very advantageous way to make provision for a child's long-term future. The only possible disadvantage is that income cannot be taken from the plan until the child's fiftieth birthday (however, this might be no bad thing).

9.27 For a baby aged one year, paying £50 (net) per month into a stakeholder pension until his eighteenth birthday could create a retirement fund of £135,000 at the age of 50, using standard industry growth rates. A Christening present of £1,000 gross (you actually pay £780 net), for a baby aged six months, paid into a stakeholder pension could create a retirement fund of over £41,000 by the time the child reached age 65.

9.28 Even via stakeholder, the impact of charges on the fund is going to be significant, since it is going to have to run for at least 50 years. A flat rate percentage charge will really bite into the funds under management in the later years.

9.29 One way round this problem is to use a SIPP which has flat annual administration fees which do not depend on the size of the fund. This will obviously be more expensive in the early years, but that will soon cease to be the case – probably from year six onwards. For simple investments a parent might deal with the fund management aspect themselves and thus avoid fund management charges. However, even if fund management charges are brought into account as well, as long as these are modest, the SIPP route will probably still produce a larger pension pot at the end of the day.

The Child Trust Fund

9.30 The government plans to introduce Child Trust Funds in 2003. In summary, the main features are:

- a centrally managed set-up process, linked to Child Benefit systems;

- progressive endowment at birth (probably £250–£500) with additional government top-ups at ages, 5, 11 and 16 (probably £100 each time);

- additional contributions – up to an annual limit – payable by parents, other family and friends, and children, with growth exempt from tax;

- investment of assets in a wide range of vehicles, including equities;

- no access to assets, including additional contributions, until account maturity;

- maturity of account at age 18;

- no restrictions to be placed on use of assets at maturity;

- financial education to be fully integrated into Child Trust Fund account through financial services providers, school curriculum and other providers;

- further consultation on role of providers of financial services in delivery of Child Trust Fund accounts.

9.31   The Child Trust Fund will certainly give a great boost to investing for children, and raise its awareness significantly among parents and grandparents.

Conclusion

9.32   The choice of investment products should be made in just the same way for a 5-year-old as a 55-year-old, based on investment objectives and attitude to risk. It should certainly not be confined to those products specifically targeted at children, although these can have their role to play.

Product opportunities

- Capital Growth Unit Trusts
- Capital Growth Investment Trusts
- Stakeholder Pensions
- SIPPs
- Children's Bonus Bonds

Chapter 10

Tax Mitigation and the Elderly

Couples and the age and married couples' allowance

10.1 As far as older couples are concerned, care should be taken to divide income-bearing assets to try and ensure that they do not lose the benefit of their higher rate personal allowance – an extra £1,485 in the case of those aged 65 to 74 years, and £1,755 for those aged 75 and over. This allowance is reduced by £1 for every £2 by which someone's net total income – after allowable deductions but before personal allowances – exceeds £17,900. However, the allowance cannot fall below the basic £4,615.

10.2 There is a further complication where the couple is entitled to a married couple's allowance. This is available only where one of the couple was born before 6 April 1935. The allowance is worth 10% of the allowance amount – £5,465 where one is aged 65 to 74 years and £5,535 if they are 75 and over. The allowance is automatically given to the husband – subject to any claim by his wife – and is reduced in exactly the same way as the higher personal allowance when the husband's income exceeds £17,900. However, the allowance can never drop below £2,110.

10.3 A married woman is entitled as of right to claim £1,055 of the married couple's allowance. Alternatively the couple may jointly claim for an allowance of twice that amount, i.e. £2,110, to be given to the wife. In either case the allowance available to the husband is reduced accordingly. Claims must be made before the beginning of the relevant tax year, e.g. before 6 April 2003 for 2003–04 (except in the year of marriage, when the claim may be made within that tax year).

10.4 Claims must be made on Form 18, available from the Inland Revenue. The allowance will then be allocated in the chosen way until the claim is withdrawn, or, where a joint claim has been made for £2,110 to go to the wife, until the husband makes a fresh claim for half of that amount. The withdrawal or the husband's claim must also be made before the beginning of the tax year for which the revised allocation is to take effect. Choosing to allocate £1,055 or £2,110 of the allowance to a wife may reduce the joint tax bill if the husband has dividend income and his tax bill would otherwise be lower than his available dividend tax credits, because such credits are not repayable.

10.5   Where this does not apply, there will be no tax saving from transferring the allowance unless the husband has insufficient income to cover the allowance, but there may be a cash flow benefit if, say, a wife pays tax under PAYE and a husband is self-employed, because the wife will start to get the benefit of the allowance at the beginning of the tax year, whereas the husband's first tax payment is due much later. If no claim is made to allocate part of the allowance to the wife, it is given to the husband.

10.6   If either husband or wife pays insufficient tax to use the married couples' allowance to which they are entitled, that spouse may notify the Revenue (not later than five years after the 31 January following the relevant tax year) that the unused amount is to be transferred to the other. The unused amount is not transferred automatically.

10.7   Those who have pension income which takes them to the limit of their age-related allowances, should consider moving money, say, a building society account into an investment bond. As we have seen, withdrawals of up to 5% per year are deemed to be return of capital and therefore generate no immediate tax liability. Thus, they will not affect the age allowances.

10.8   The capital is, of course, not as safe as in the building society, but there is also potential for capital growth. Also, when the bond is cashed in, the whole of the gain will be used to determine any entitlement to age-related allowances. Top-slicing relief is not available for this purpose. Almost inevitably, therefore, age-related allowances will be lost in the tax year when the bond is encashed.

Power of attorney

10.9   Most people require the freedom to deal with their own money and handle their own financial affairs in privacy. However, there may come a time when a person can no longer remain independent and they may then need help either on a temporary or permanent basis. Taking control over another person's money or property is a serious matter which should not be taken lightly. It is important that control is never taken away from people against their wishes if they are still able to manage for themselves.

10.10 Many arrangements can be made informally without the need for any legal approval. These include authorisation to use someone else's bank or building society account by mandate, putting money into a joint account and appointing someone as an agent, say to collect social security benefits or pensions. A 'third party' mandate is required to authorise one person to use another person's bank or building society account. Requirements vary but in many cases a signed letter of authority is sufficient. Such a mandate ceases if the actual account holder becomes mentally incapable.

10.11 The advantages of a joint account are that either or any of the holders have easy access to the funds and if one dies the balance on the account immediately passes to the other holder or holders. Problems can arise if account holders disagree or if one becomes mentally incapacitated, when the account may be frozen until new arrangements are made. In the case of social security benefits or pensions the declaration on the back of the payment slip can be signed to authorise payment to an agent. If this is likely to be an on-going situation a claimant can ask the Benefits Agency office to issue a card.

10.12 More formally, a person may grant an enduring power of attorney. This is a deed that enables donors, while still mentally capable, to appoint an attorney, usually a close relative or friend, either to take over their affairs at once and continue to act when they become mentally incapable, or to act as attorney only when the donor is no longer mentally capable of acting for themselves. Such a power must be drawn up using a three-part form which is available from law stationers.

10.13 Donors must state whether they wish their attorney to have full authority or if they wish to put limitations on the power. In this latter case it would be wise to seek legal advice. Once a donor starts to become mentally incapacitated the enduring power must be registered with the Public Trust Office. Prior to this the donor and their near relatives must be given notice of intention to register. Before registration an enduring power can be revoked by the donor at any time while still mentally capable.

10.14 If a person becomes incapable of looking after their own affairs and has not made any previous arrangements, such as making an enduring power of attorney, it may be necessary to act without their consent or even against their wishes. If the person concerned has a large income and considerable savings it will be necessary to apply to the Court of Protection to take over the management of their financial affairs.

10.15   This whole process will take some time and in the case of extreme urgency the Court can use any of its powers before the necessary medical evidence is available without having to notify the patient or others. It is much more straightforward to deal with a person's affairs when they become mentally incapacitated if they have set up an enduring power of attorney whilst still in full command of their faculties.

Equity release schemes

10.16   There are a variety of schemes available, but they all boil down to the same thing. A sum of money is realised on an elderly person's house by means of a mortgage, and this sum is either paid over to the individual or used to buy an annuity.

10.17   This is probably a case where simplest is best – a capital sum paid to the individual. This route can usually avoid any loss of the age-related allowances due to income going over the £17,900 threshold.

10.18   A good scheme will have the following characteristics:

* interest on loan fixed at outset for the whole loan period;
* the ability to make further releases of capital;
* loan interest rolled up until property finally sold;
* a guarantee that a negative equity situation will never arise.

10.19   The only setback here is that it is uncertain how much must be paid back at the end, although the overall payment will be capped with a decent plan. This capping will be of particular advantage to those who live a long time.

Long-term care

10.20   Under the *Community Care Act*, Local Authorities are legally obliged to help with care fees for elderly people who do not have enough money to pay their own fees. If a person's assets are less than £18,500, the Local Authority is duty bound to assess the ability to pay for care but it should be noted that different authorities have different rates.

10.21   Although someone may not qualify for financial assistance immediately, they might qualify in the future. It is therefore advisable to involve the Local Authority from the outset.

10.22   Local Authorities do have far-reaching powers to take into account any money that they believe has been deliberately given away in order to qualify for State assistance.

10.23   The government has introduced a nursing care allowance for those already in care. This is a fixed amount but various conditions have to be met to receive the maximum. Broadly, the NHS pays for nursing care but domiciliary and convalescent care is means tested. The difficulty often is to establish which is which and thus who will pay for what.

10.24   The value of any residential property will usually be counted as capital, but the value of the family home or normal residence may be excluded in specific circumstances. The value of the family home is not counted as part of an individual's capital for the first 12 weeks after entering care.

10.25   Insurance based products are available to help towards the cost of care and a number of types are being marketed. The future cost of care is not easily quantified but insurance can be taken out to fund a forecast level of care based on a monthly amount. A claim is made once the insured is diagnosed with a mental impairment, such as Alzheimer's, and/or fails two or more activities of daily living (ADL).

10.26   Alternatively a lump sum investment can be made to a special long-term care fund, which usually consists of shares or unit trusts. Regular monthly deductions are then made from the bond to cover the cost of insuring for the long-term care benefit selected. If a claim is not made, the investment can then be passed to named beneficiaries on death.

10.27   In certain circumstances an immediate needs annuity might be the answer. To qualify for an immediate needs annuity, the individual should be in or about to enter a care home or require domiciliary care as a result of a medical condition.

10.28   This special type of annuity pays an enhanced income direct to the care provider for the life of the annuitant. As with all annuities, the capital is invested in exchange for an income, so there are no further payments after the death of the policyholder. Once the annuity is purchased, the capital that has been invested is gone forever.

10.29   The amount of the annuity will depend on age, gender, and state of health, and is usually aligned to an assessment system called the Anderton Diagnosis Index. This primarily assesses the severity of the applicant's condition and combines it with their ability to perform certain ADLs.

Product opportunities

- Single Premium Investment Bonds
- Equity Release Mortgages
- Long-term Care Insurance
- Long-term Care Fund
- Immediate Needs Annuities

Chapter 11

Tax Aspects of a Relationship Breakdown

Introduction

11.1   In the UK, the rate of divorce is on the increase and over one third of marriages end up on the rocks. The same is presumably true of relationships where a couple simply cohabit. However, the tax and legal implications can be quite different.

Divorce and income tax

11.2   The only relevance from a personal allowance point of view is for those couples who are entitled to the married couple's allowance. Depending on age this is worth either £546.50 or £553.50 in hard cash terms. It is given in full in the year of separation, but is not available after that.

11.3   A person separated from their spouse who has a child under 16 living with them may claim the children's tax credit, which is worth £529 in hard cash terms in the current year.

11.4   As far as maintenance is concerned, with limited exception where one spouse was 65 before 5 April 2000, there is no income tax relief. Even then, it is tax-free to the recipient.

Divorce and CGT

11.5   CGT can be an important consideration when a marriage breaks down and the sooner the parties agree on the division of any capital assets the better. CGT is payable at an individual's highest rate of tax on any gain realised on most assets. For CGT the important year is the tax year in which the couple separate and not the tax year in which the divorce proceedings start or end. Transfers of assets between spouses at any time during the year of separation are not chargeable provided both are resident in the UK. The spouse receiving the asset simply takes it over at original cost.

11.6   In some cases, however, it may be better to arrange for any transfers of capital assets to be made in the period between 6 April following the date of separation and the date of the decree absolute. Transfers during this period are treated as being made at open market value. This is of advantage to the recipient, because any capital gain arising on a subsequent disposal will be lower than if it had been transferred at cost in the year of separation.

11.7   The spouse transferring the asset in these circumstances will of course suffer a capital gain based on the difference between the original cost of the asset and its market value at date of transfer. However, it is often possible to avoid tax here by using the annual CGT exemption allowance.

11.8   Frequently the only capital asset to be transferred in divorce proceedings is the former matrimonial home or an interest in it. The person making the transfer is entitled to claim the relief from CGT which is due on a principal private residence (PPR). However, depending how property prices have moved, it may be better for the transferor to elect to treat any new house as their PPR right from the date of its acquisition. Although this may give rise to a capital gain on the former matrimonial home, the departing spouse is considered to be in occupation of it for the last three years of their ownership even if they are also claiming PPR relief on another house for that period. Therefore, any capital gain on the former matrimonial home in those three years will escape CGT as will any gain on the new home.

Divorce and IHT

11.9   Transfers between husband and wife are exempt for IHT purposes. This exemption exists up to the time when a decree absolute is issued. In many cases, therefore, there is no need to worry about IHT implications for transfers of assets and lump sum payments, as long as they are made before the decree absolute is issued. Transfers after that date could possibly give rise to an IHT liability if the transferor dies within seven years of the date of the transfer. There are, however, various other IHT exemptions and reliefs available for transfers made after the decree absolute.

11.10   For instance, there are unlikely to be any IHT problems if a transfer is made between a divorced couple to give effect to some provision which has been agreed. A problem can arise where a guilty conscience leads to unusual generosity by one of the parties. If a former spouse has not made any demand for additional provision, such largesse is not exempt from IHT.

11.11   Again, there are no IHT problems with payments for the maintenance of the other party to a marriage or former marriage. A transfer is also exempt from IHT if it is made as normal expenditure, and out of income, and leaving sufficient to maintain the transferor's usual standard of living.

11.12   There is no exemption as such for IHT purposes in respect of gifts to children. There is exemption for payments made to a child specifically for maintenance, education or training. However, beyond the age of 18, the exemption can continue only if a child is continuously in full-time education or training. Payments for part-time training after 18 are not exempt from IHT provisions. It should also be noted that if a person ceases full-time education, takes up a job and then, say, a year or two after reaching 18 resumes full-time education, there would be no IHT relief. However, a gap year between school and university would probably be regarded as temporary.

Cohabitation and relationship breakdown

11.13   We turn now to cohabitation. When a relationship breaks down a spouse is in a much better legal position than a cohabitant. This is because on the property front, married couples can rely on the *Matrimonial Causes Act 1973* to ensure fair treatment. This means that a spouse has an automatic right to claim maintenance, capital, and a share in property and any pension fund. In the case of cohabitation, there is no right to claim maintenance or capital.

11.14   The Law Commission itself concedes that trying to establish a share in an ex-cohabitant's property is an unfair, uncertain and illogical process. Even if a couple have children there is no right to maintenance. Any property transferred to the mother as a home has to be sold once the children are 18 or leave university. The sale proceeds go to the father.

11.15   Any assets on death will pass according to the laws of intestacy if an individual does not have a will. A will is necessary to ensure that any assets go to their cohabitee and dependants as planned.

11.16   There are some tax advantages of cohabitation. These include:

- If cohabitees are not also business partners and one sells an asset to the other at a price below open market value, it is at least arguable that the disposal proceeds for (CGT) purposes should be the actual sale price.

- If cohabitees each have total ownership of separate houses with no equitable ownership in the other's house, tax law seems to be worded as to allow each to claim principal private residence relief on their own house. Any capital gain on either will thus escape CGT.

- Transfer of assets between cohabitees is deemed to be at open market value. Thus assets can be transferred from one to another to use up the transferor's annual exempt amount of £7,700 and a higher base cost for the asset has been established, thus reducing any capital gain on the eventual sale.

- There are many anti-avoidance provisions where a company director gives benefits to a spouse but, with the exception of company car rules, these provisions do not normally apply to cohabitee benefits.

11.17   The main tax disadvantages of cohabitation include:

- Transfer of assets between cohabitees can give rise to a CGT charge if the transferor has already utilised their exempt amount.

- When computing CGT taper relief on the eventual disposal of any asset which has been transferred between cohabitees, the recipient cannot add the donor's period of ownership to their own.

- On the death of one cohabitee, there is no IHT exemption on the transfer of assets to the survivor. Estate planning may, therefore, be more important than for spouses.

- Lifetime transfers of assets between cohabitees will only be potentially exempt for IHT purposes so that some IHT may become payable if the transferor dies within seven years.

Index